How to Walk on the MOON

And Other Incredible Ideas About Physics

William Potter

Richard Watson

ARCTURUS

ARCTURUS

This edition published in 2024 by Arcturus Publishing Limited
26/27 Bickels Yard, 151-153 Bermondsey Street,
London SE1 3HA

Author: William Potter
Illustrator: Richard Watson
Editor: Lydia Halliday
Consultant: Robert Snedden
Designers: Sarah and Noel Fountain
Managing Designer: Rosie Bellwood-Moyler
Managing Editor: Joe Harris

ISBN: 978-1-3988-4372-1
CH011587US
Supplier 29, Date 0724, PI 0007360

Printed in China

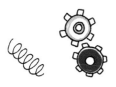

Contents

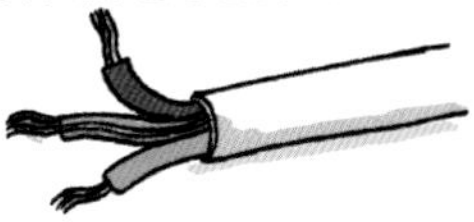

PROFESSOR ALBERT KATZENSTEIN'S
Foreword to

Welcome! I'm Professor Albert Katzenstein, here to introduce you to the wonderful world of physics.

AHEM

And this is my eager young lab assistant, Scooter the guinea pig.

Pleasure to meet you.

I've been fascinated by science since I was a kitten.

I remember the first time I fell out of a tree and discovered gravity.

Are you *sure* you discovered gravity?

Through study and experiments, scientists like me have discovered a lot about how our world and the greater Universe works.

I helped, too.

I'd like to share what I've learned with you.

If you want to know how to build a rocket, move at super speeds, and, indeed, how to walk on the Moon, you're in the right place.

Yay!

Physics, like all branches of science, is about looking for the answers to difficult questions. And we've got lots of answers for you.

What is physics?

Good question, Scooter!

What is Physics?

Physics is the branch of science concerned with the properties of matter, motion, energy, and force. That means we'll be looking at electricity, heat, light ...

Scooter, don't look directly at that lamp, you'll damage your eyes!

Is physics useful?

Very. Physics has helped us design engines for cars, invent smartphones, fly through the air, build towering skyscrapers, and send satellites into orbit.

Physics also helps us find new sources of energy to power our gadgets and vehicles, and to keep the lights on.

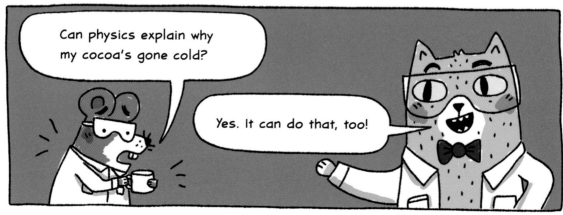

Can physics explain why my cocoa's gone cold?

Yes. It can do that, too!

Super Powers

(Energy and Forces)

How to Be a Weightlifter

GNNNNRRRR ...

Do you need help, Scooter?

Nrrrr ... no, I got this ...

GASP!

THUMP!

You could make this so much easier with a pulley.

Could you pulley this weight off of me?

I'm doing it! I'm superstrong!

Pulleys have made light work of this!

Oh ...

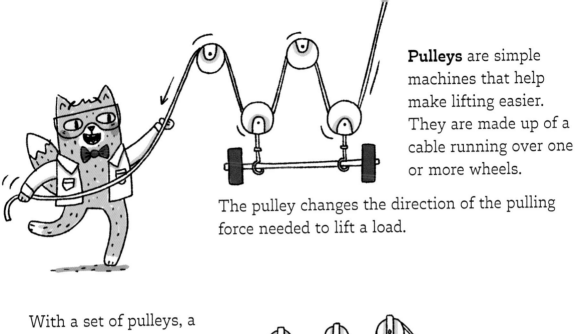

Pulleys are simple machines that help make lifting easier. They are made up of a cable running over one or more wheels.

The pulley changes the direction of the pulling force needed to lift a load.

With a set of pulleys, a weak pulling force over a long distance becomes a strong pulling force over a short distance.

Using a longer cable over two wheels can halve the effort needed to lift a load. Using four wheels means that you only need about a quarter of the pulling force.

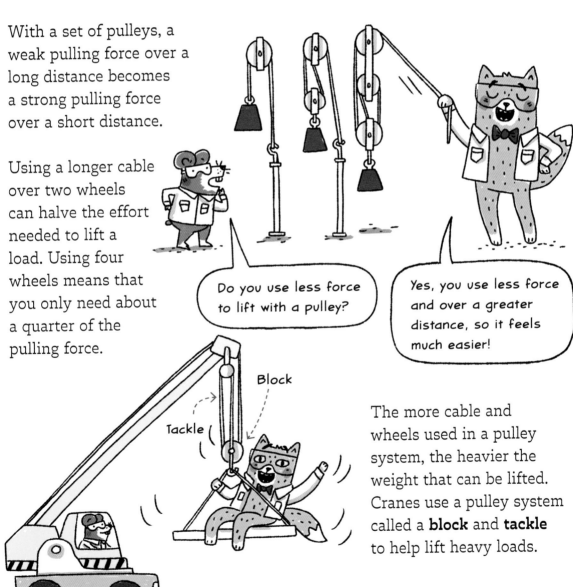

Do you use less force to lift with a pulley?

Yes, you use less force and over a greater distance, so it feels much easier!

Block

Tackle

The more cable and wheels used in a pulley system, the heavier the weight that can be lifted. Cranes use a pulley system called a **block** and **tackle** to help lift heavy loads.

How to Balance on a Seesaw

HELP!

I can't reach the ground.

You're too heavy to join me on the seesaw.

I'll have you know I am the ideal weight for my height.

And balance is not a problem.

If I just shuffle closer to the seesaw's pivot ...

A little more ...

That better for you?

BOING!

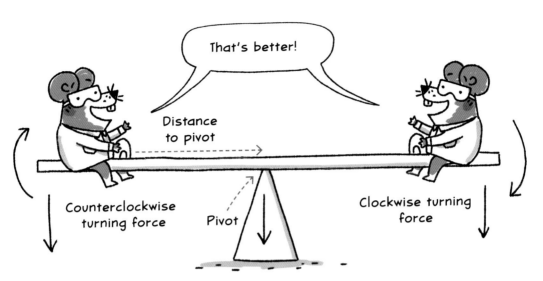

The weight of people on a seesaw creates a **downward force**, which turns the seesaw around its pivot. When the turning forces at each end are equal but in opposite directions, the seesaw is balanced.

The turning effect of a force is called the **moment** of the force. The moment is calculated by multiplying the turning force by the distance from the pivot.

The farther a person sits from the pivot, the greater the moment they create, and their end of the seesaw will move downward. If they move closer to the pivot, they produce less of a turning force, and their end rises.

How to Crack a Hard Nut

Nut.

EXCUSE ME!

NUT. Would you like a WALNUT?

Oh, thank you!

URRRGH ...

Careful! You'll break your teeth!

Why don't you try using this?

!

SIGH

PAK!

12

Nutcrackers are not to be used as hammers.

Nutcrackers are a **force multiplier**. They convert a weak force over a long distance into a strong force over a short distance. A light squeeze on the handles becomes a hard squeeze around the nut.

They work as a pair of **levers**, or rigid bars, that move around a fixed point called a **fulcrum**. The nut fits between the levers. When the levers are squeezed together, they press on the nut, causing its shell to crack open.

Other kinds of levers include pliers, wrenches, and bottle openers.

A NUTCRACKER

Fulcrum

Effort

Load

Fzzzz!

Oops!

All Kinds of Energy

Energy has been around since the beginning of the Universe. It's what makes things happen, from lighting a room, to warming up a cup of cocoa.

Mmm, cocoa!

Energy can change from one form to another, but can never be created or destroyed. Here are the key types of energy...

Chemical
This is energy stored in the bonds between atoms and released through chemical reactions. Chemical energy is held in batteries, fuel, and food.

Kinetic
Kinetic energy is stored in a moving object. This depends on the object's speed and mass. The faster an object moves or the greater its mass, the more kinetic energy.

Gravitational
This is the energy of an object above the Earth's surface. The amount of an object's potential energy depends on its position.

Elastic

This is the potential energy held in an elastic object, such as a spring, when it is compressed or stretched. The energy is released when the elastic object springs back to its original shape.

Acoustic

Sound energy is made when an object, such as a guitar string, vibrates.

Radiant

All objects give off radiant energy, carried by electromagnetic waves such as light, radio waves, or X-rays.

Electrical

Electrical energy is the movement of electrons, which can pass through a wire as electricity, or hit the ground as lightning.

Thermal

Heat energy is produced by vibrating atoms in a substance. The faster they vibrate, the hotter the substance becomes.

Magnetic

This is the energy stored in the magnetic field surrounding two magnets that attract or repel each other.

Nuclear

Stored in atoms, nuclear energy is released when the atoms are fused together or split apart through nuclear fusion or fission.

How to Put a Spring in Your Step

Scooter, you look rather tired.

I had to stay up all night monitoring your paint-drying experiment.

Oh, that...

Never mind. I know how to put a spring back in your step!

These spring shoes will have you bouncing about the room.

I'm not sure...

Wow! These are great!

I wonder how high I could go...

BOING

Take it easy, Scooter. One small step at a time...

I can almost touch the ceiling!

BOING

BONK

BONK

OW! OW! Turn them off!

BOING

BOING

BONK

Another great leap for science!

A spring is an elastic object that returns to its original shape when stretched, compressed, or bent.

Stretching or compressing a spring gives it elastic potential energy that will pull it back to its original position.

The stretch of a spring is proportional to the stretching force applied to it. This is **Hooke's Law**. If a weight stretches a spring by one length, twice the weight will stretch it by twice the length.

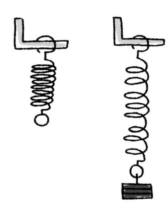

Springs are useful for measuring forces. A **force meter** has a spring inside. When it is used to pull an object, the spring is stretched, pulling a marker along a scale to give a measure in **Newtons** (N), the units for measuring forces.

Springs are used in many things, such as scales, mattresses, and mountain bike suspensions.

Force meter

How to Stay Afloat

It's not time for my annual bath. You know I don't like to get my fur wet.

This isn't bath time. It's an experiment.

A rubber duck floats on water, but how about a metal duck?

CAREFUL! It will sink and bump my feet!

It's floating! But how?! Metal is heavier than water!

It is, but the metal duck is hollow, so its average density is less than water.

Call me dense, but why did I need to be in the water for you to test this?

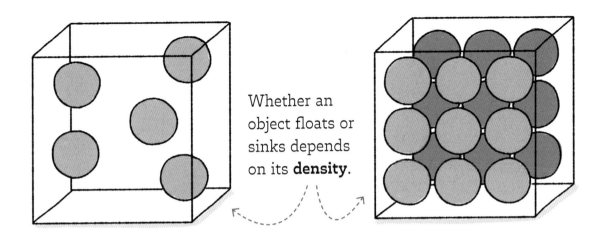

Whether an object floats or sinks depends on its **density**.

Density is how much mass is contained in an object. Steel is denser than wood. Wood is denser than air.

Density = Mass/Volume

For an object to float in water, its average density needs to be less than that of water. While a metal coin may be denser and sink, a metal ship is full of air so its average density is less than water.

Upthrust

A boat floats because of a force called **upthrust**. This upward force is equal to the weight of the water that the boat displaces. If the weight of the boat is less than the upthrust, it will float.

How to Dive Deep

AAAARGHHH!

Calm down, Scooter. Everything's under control.

But ... **SCARY FISH!!!!**

You're perfectly safe in my paws.

And nothing's going to get through this window—the glass is as thick as a brick.

Why so thick?

Down here in the deepest ocean, the water pressure can be hundreds of times more than on the surface. That's because of the weight of all that water above us.

If you went outside, all the gases in your body would be quickly compressed. You'd be squashed!

GULP!

How come the fish aren't squished?

Because they don't have air inside their bodies. They are mostly water, which can't easily be compressed.

I still feel under pressure. Can we return to the surface?

I can control this submersible to go up and down at any time.

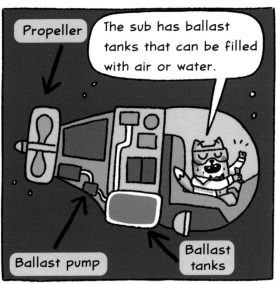

Propeller

The sub has ballast tanks that can be filled with air or water.

Ballast pump

Ballast tanks

To dive, I let water into the tanks, increasing the sub's average density.

To surface, I pump air into the tanks, reducing the sub's average density.

With all this up and down, I think last night's dinner is ready to surface, too!

How to Measure a Shark

I've got my ruler! What did you say we're measuring today?

I'll show you.

WAUGH! It's a shark! How did you get that in the lab?

I brought him in.

May I introduce highly respected naturalist, Dr. Rosie Ringtail.

IT'S A SHARK! A SHARK!

I see you know your fish, Mr. Scooter.

Today we're going to measure the shark's volume.

I'm not getting in that tank!

You won't need to, and you won't need that ruler, either!

This crane will safely lift the shark into a new tank of water.

And we shall measure the volume of the shark using water displacement.

How much the water level rises tells us the shark's volume.

Couldn't you measure my goldfish instead?

Volume is the measure of how much space an object takes up.

For a simple shape like a cube, you can measure the length of each side to find out its volume.

Length x Width x Height = Volume

But for a complex shape, you can use the water displacement method.

A submerged object displaces a volume of liquid that matches its own volume.

Goldie has grown this week!

So, if you drop an orange into a pitcher of water and measure the difference in water level, that's the volume of the orange.

How to Become Taller

NRRRRGH ...

You sound like you're in pain.

I'm just doing my stretches.

Me, too!

I didn't know you were into yoga.

I'm not. I'm doing some stretching and compression tests.

Can I be stretched to become taller?

Every material can be stretched or compressed by some amount when you supply the right amount of force.

Like this piece of toffee, for example.

Is that from my secret toffee stash?

Um, I think I'm the perfect size for a guinea pig, actually.

All solids can be stretched or compressed to some degree by using force. The change of shape is called **deformation**.

If an object springs back to its original shape after the force is removed, this is called **elastic deformation**. If the object stays stretched or compressed, this is called **plastic deformation**.

An elastic band shrinks back after stretching, so this is **elastic deformation**.

A squashed soda bottle stays squashed, so this is **plastic deformation**.

I'm an elastic guinea pig!

Brittle materials, such as glass and ceramics, break very quickly if stretched or compressed.

Elastic materials have an elastic limit from which they will not spring back. If a spring is stretched to this limit, it will no longer act as a spring.

The disks between human backbones or vertebra act like a spring and are compressed by gravity. After a night's sleep, you might gain a tiny amount in height as the disks between your vertebrae stretch out, but once you're up they become compressed again, and you shrink.

How to See in the Dark

Oops. That last experiment caused a fuse to blow.

Can you find the fuse box, Scooter?

Scooter?

BUMP

I think I walked into a table.

That wasn't a table. That was me.

How can we find the fuse box in the dark?

I have a bright idea.

So you have!

Now, let's get the power back on...

...and return to my experiment...

Wait!

FZZZT!

Oops.

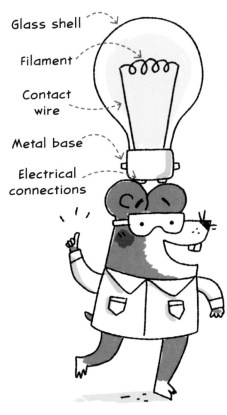

Glass shell

Filament

Contact wire

Metal base

Electrical connections

Two ways of producing electric light are:

Incandescence, which heats an object until it glows.

Luminescence, which produces light without heating.

An **incandescent light bulb** produces light when it is connected to an electrical circuit. The electric current passes through a thin wire called a **filament** inside a glass shell.

This filament can reach a high temperature without melting. It glows as it warms up, releasing light energy.

An incandescent bulb produces heat as well as light energy, so it is not very energy efficient and does not last long.

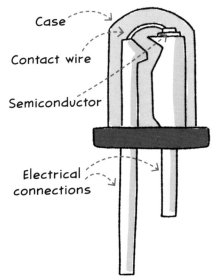

Case

Contact wire

Semiconductor

Electrical connections

An LED (light-emitting diode) is a **luminescent** light source. It uses less electricity to give off light.

LEDs do not have filaments. They use a special material called a semiconductor that gives off light when a current passes through it.

LEDs are used to light rooms and for television screens.

How to Avoid a Soaking

Here you go, Scooter.

I want you to turn this bucket upside down without spilling any water.

You're joking, right?

It's a serious experiment.

I don't see *you* getting wet for science...

Listen carefully. You need to swing the bucket in a circle at a good speed.

How will that help...?

Amazing! The bucket is turning upside down, but no water falls out!

That's because of centripetal force.

Centipede what?!

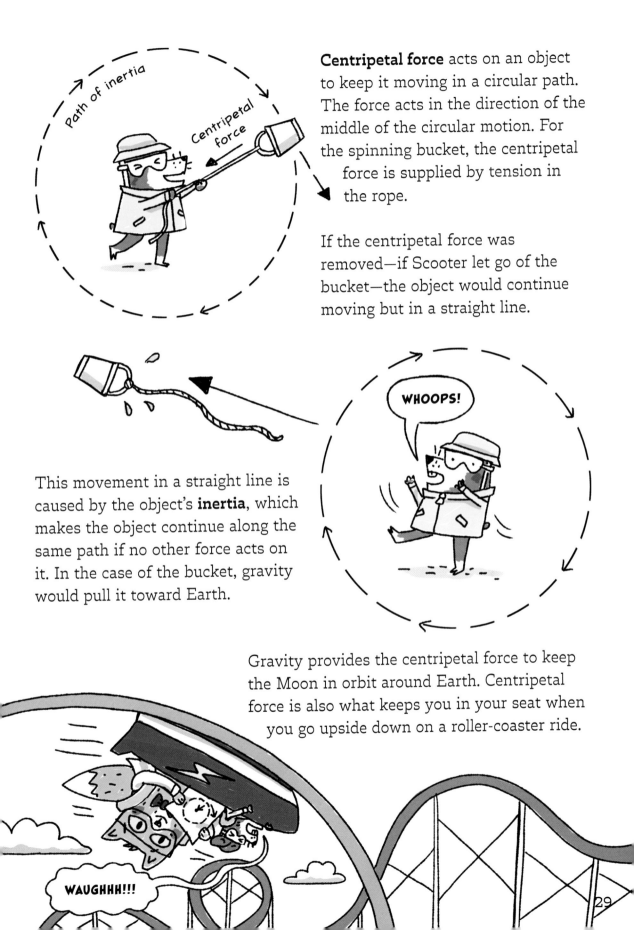

Centripetal force acts on an object to keep it moving in a circular path. The force acts in the direction of the middle of the circular motion. For the spinning bucket, the centripetal force is supplied by tension in the rope.

If the centripetal force was removed—if Scooter let go of the bucket—the object would continue moving but in a straight line.

This movement in a straight line is caused by the object's **inertia**, which makes the object continue along the same path if no other force acts on it. In the case of the bucket, gravity would pull it toward Earth.

Gravity provides the centripetal force to keep the Moon in orbit around Earth. Centripetal force is also what keeps you in your seat when you go upside down on a roller-coaster ride.

Path of inertia

Centripetal force

WHOOPS!

WAUGHHH!!!

29

How to Split an Atom

CATCH!

What's this?

It's the nucleus of a uranium atom.

Uranium?! Isn't that radioactive? That's why you're wearing protective gear!

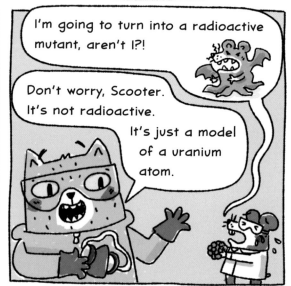

I'm going to turn into a radioactive mutant, aren't I?!

Don't worry, Scooter. It's not radioactive.

It's just a model of a uranium atom.

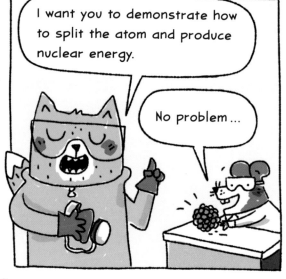

I want you to demonstrate how to split the atom and produce nuclear energy.

No problem...

STOP! You don't split an atom with an ax!

Matter is made up of tiny atoms that are made up of smaller particles called protons, neutrons, and electrons. Protons and neutrons are in the nucleus of the atom.

Uranium is a radioactive material with a nucleus that can split apart, releasing a lot of energy.

Nucleus splits into smaller nuclei and neutrons

Neutrons hit more uranium nuclei, starting a chain reaction

Uranium nucleus

Neutron

This atom splitting is called **nuclear fission**. In nuclear power plants, the process is controlled to produce a series of fission events called a **chain reaction**. The heat released is used to create steam to drive turbines and generate electricity.

While nuclear fission produces much energy, it also produces harmful radioactive waste which has to be safely stored for thousands of years.

Another way of producing energy from atoms is **nuclear fusion**, which fuses rather than splits nuclei. This can create energy without radioactive waste.

The process is very difficult to produce on Earth, but it could become a future clean energy source.

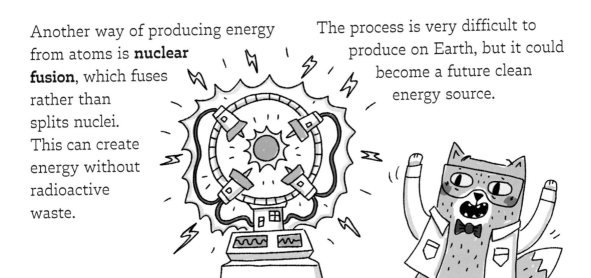

Power Points

We need energy to heat and light our homes, power our computers, and fuel our vehicles. This energy comes from many sources. Some are nonrenewable, which means they will eventually run out. Some are renewable, which means they are continually restored.

FOSSIL FUELS

Fossil fuels are a nonrenewable energy source that comes from the fossilized remains of plants and animals.

Oil (**petroleum**) and **natural gas** are produced from the remains of tiny buried prehistoric plants and sea creatures. Oil is drilled for, then pumped to the surface. It then goes to a refinery to be turned into fuel.

I'm feeling the heat and pressure, too!

WHOOPS!

Natural gas is often found near oil deposits and is piped away for storage before being used as a fuel for heating and cooking.

Burning fossil fuels produces a greenhouse gas called carbon dioxide. This increases the effect of global warming, raising temperatures in the air and oceans, so efforts are being made to use renewable energy sources instead.

RENEWABLE ENERGY

Solar Power

Light from the Sun is converted into electrical energy using solar panels. Panels can be placed on the roofs of buildings, or in fields.

Wind Power

The blades of tall turbines are turned by the wind. This converts kinetic energy into electrical energy. Wind farms with many turbines can be found on land or at sea.

Water Power

Moving water has kinetic energy. Hydroelectric dams are often built to create reservoirs. When the water is released through the dam, it can be used to spin turbines and generate electricity.

Geothermal

In areas with hot springs and volcanic activity, hot water and steam can be piped out of the ground to turn turbines and generate electricity.

Nuclear Power

Nuclear energy is produced through nuclear fission. This produces a lot of energy but also creates radioactive waste.

BIOFUEL

Biofuel is produced from the **biomass** of plants, algae, and even dung. It is considered a renewable energy source because plants and animal feed can be harvested, then replanted.

Biodiesel is a biofuel that can be made from soybean, oil palm, or recycled cooking oil.

Methane and **biogas** can be produced from decomposing biomass, such as food waste.

Wood is a biofuel that can be burned to produce the heat to run generators.

Ethanol is a liquid biofuel made from corn (maize) or sugarcane.

Going Through the Motions

(Forces and Motion)

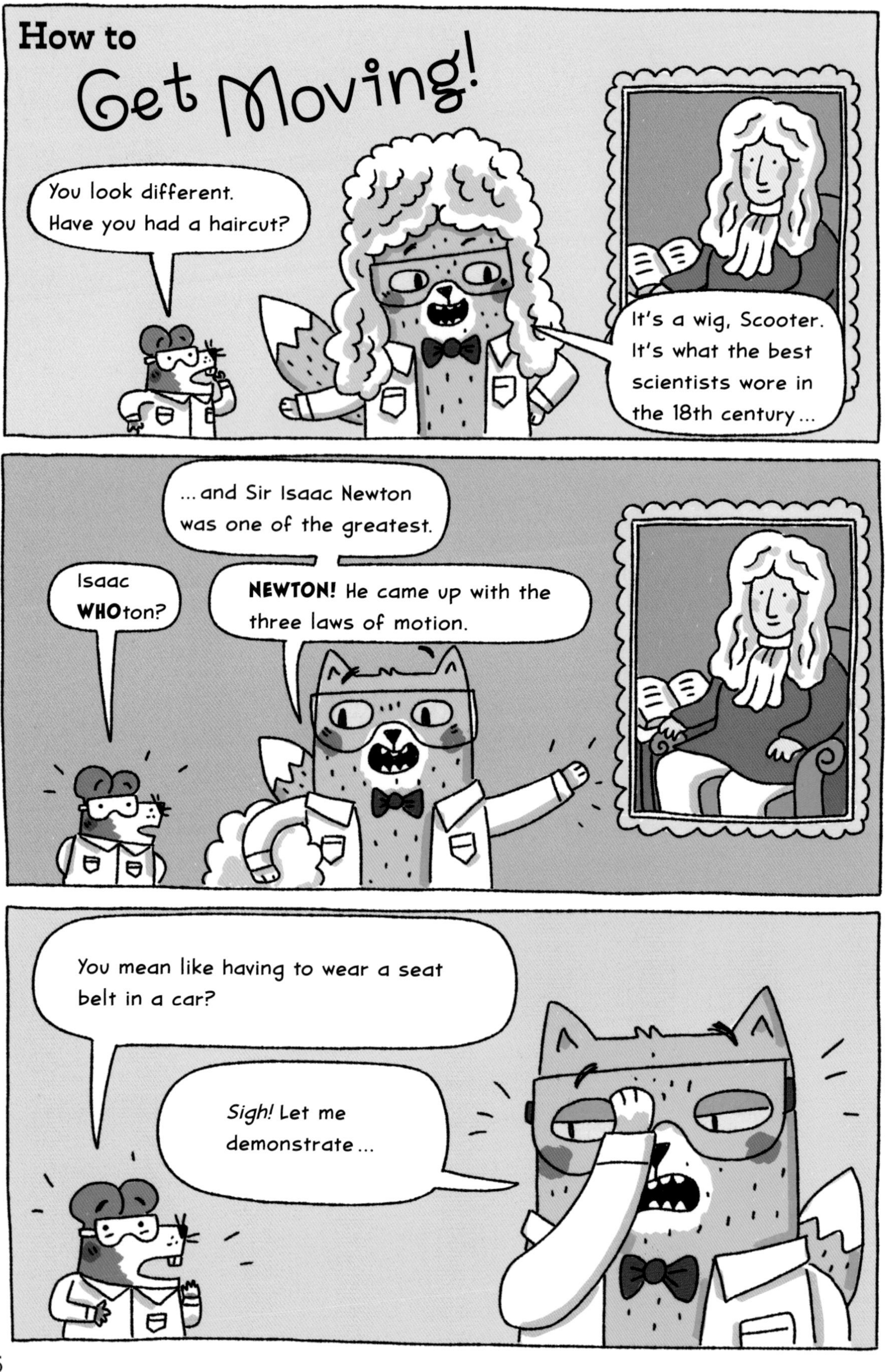
How to Get Moving!
You look different. Have you had a haircut?
It's a wig, Scooter. It's what the best scientists wore in the 18th century ...
... and Sir Isaac Newton was one of the greatest.
Isaac WHOton?
NEWTON! He came up with the three laws of motion.
You mean like having to wear a seat belt in a car?
Sigh! Let me demonstrate ...

Newton's Laws of Motion

Issac Newton set out his laws of motion in 1687.

Newton's first law of motion states that an object remains at rest or moving in a straight line at constant speed unless acted on by a force.

Newton's second law states that an object's acceleration depends on its mass and the amount of force applied.

Newton's third law states that to every action, there is an equal and opposite reaction.

Reaction / Action

Who was Isaac Newton?

Issac Newton was an English mathematician and physicist who lived from 1642 to 1727.

CRONCH!

Newton is famous for explaining gravity, an idea said to have come to him when he saw an apple fall from a tree.

Newton also investigated the refraction of light through a prism and invented the reflecting telescope.

How to Build a Rocket

Bye!

Where are you off to?

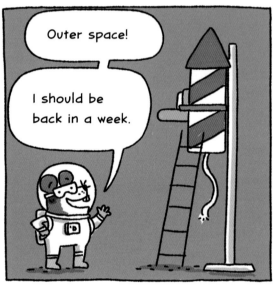

Outer space!

I should be back in a week.

You'll be back in just a few seconds if you try launching yourself with this firework!

Firework? It said it was a rocket on the packet.

It's designed to go "bang" not carry you into space.

Oh. Can you build me a proper rocket then...?

It would be a shame to waste all the sandwiches I prepared.

Rockets carry a fuel called **propellant**, which is burned in a **combustion chamber**, releasing hot gas. The gas leaves exhaust nozzles at high speed and pushes the rocket up, against the force of gravity and air **drag**. This directional force is called **thrust**.

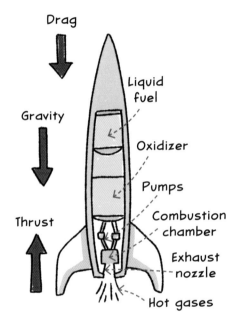

Drag

Gravity

Thrust

Liquid fuel

Oxidizer

Pumps

Combustion chamber

Exhaust nozzle

Hot gases

On Earth, fuels need the gas **oxygen** to burn. With no oxygen in space, rockets carry a liquid **oxidizer** to ignite the fuel.

As the fuel burns, the mass of the rocket is reduced, so the same thrust has a greater effect, and the rocket's speed increases. Rockets carry fuel in booster tanks that can be detached. They drop back to Earth during launch to reduce the the rocket's mass even more.

Following **Newton's third law of motion**, the force of the hot gas leaving the exhaust is balanced by the thrust pushing the rocket in the opposite direction. The exhaust does not need land or air to push against in oredr to propel the rocket.

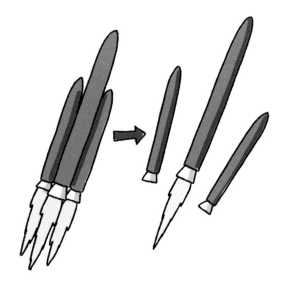

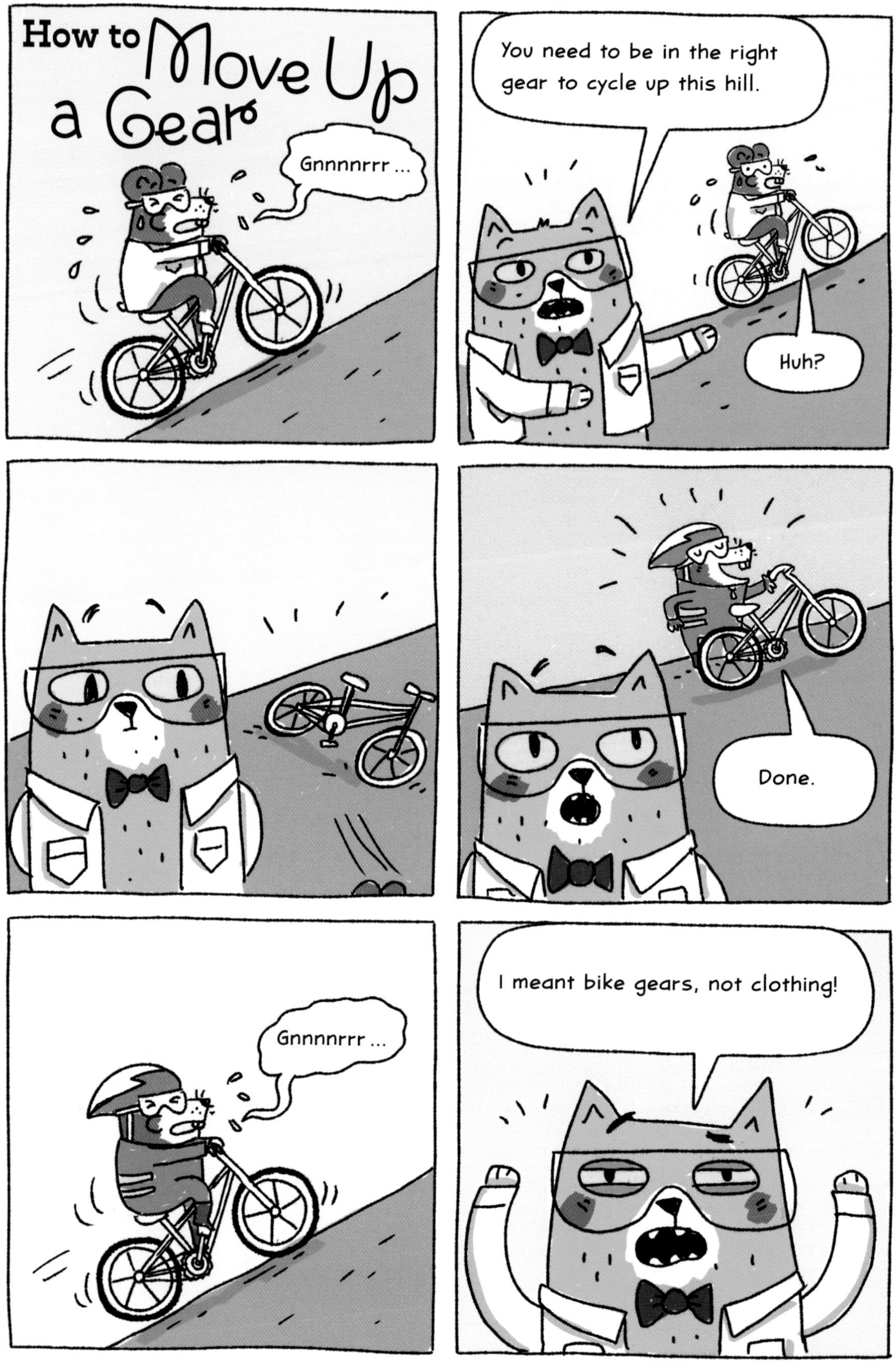
How to Move Up a Gear
Gnnnnrrr ...
You need to be in the right gear to cycle up this hill.
Huh?
Done.
Gnnnnrrr ...
I meant bike gears, not clothing!

Gears are toothed wheels that lock together. Turning one wheel turns the wheel it is connected to as well.

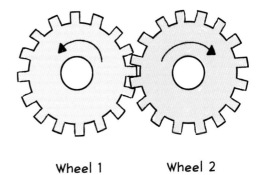

If wheels 1 and 2 are the same size, with the same number of teeth, a complete turn of wheel 1 turns wheel 2 by a complete turn, too.

Wheel 1   Wheel 2

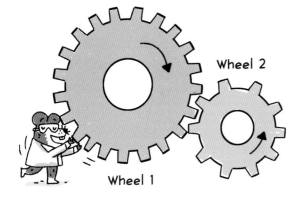

Wheel 2

Wheel 1

If wheel 2 is smaller, a complete turn of wheel 1 will turn wheel 2 more than one turn, meaning that it rotates faster.

On a bike, a chain connects the pedals and **chainring** with the gears on the rear wheel. When you change gears, you move the chain between different gear wheels, which controls your speed.

LOW GEAR

Rear gear wheels

Chainring

HIGH GEAR

Rotation of rear wheel

Turning force

When using a **low gear**, the **turning force** of one pedal stroke rotates the rear wheel a short distance. The bike will move slowly.

When using a **high gear**, the turning force of one pedal stroke rotates the rear wheel a longer distance. This is used for bicycling fast.

How to Keep on Going

Are you ready, Scooter?

I don't know how to rollerblade!

You'll soon get the hang of it.

The force of my push has given you **MOTION**. Your mass and speed give you **MOMENTUM**.

But how will I stop?

You won't, unless another force acts on you, or you have a collision.

COLLISION?!!

CRASH!

I think I lost my momentum.

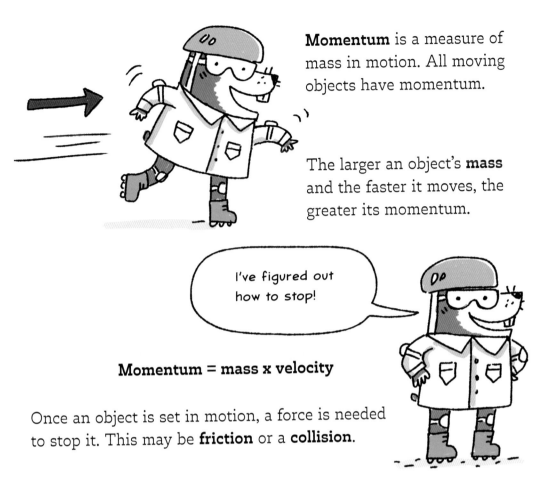

Momentum is a measure of mass in motion. All moving objects have momentum.

The larger an object's **mass** and the faster it moves, the greater its momentum.

I've figured out how to stop!

Momentum = mass x velocity

Once an object is set in motion, a force is needed to stop it. This may be **friction** or a **collision**.

Whoa!

If a moving object hits another object, it may transfer some of its momentum and set the other object in motion, too. Momentum is always conserved, so the momentum of both moving objects equals the momentum of the first object before the collision.

Both objects will eventually stop moving, however, since forces such as friction and air resistance act on them.

How to Reach Terminal Velocity

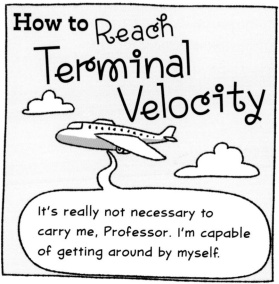

It's really not necessary to carry me, Professor. I'm capable of getting around by myself.

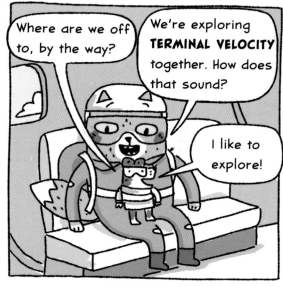

Where are we off to, by the way?

We're exploring **TERMINAL VELOCITY** together. How does that sound?

I like to explore!

Now, just put these on...

When do we land?

Oh, very, very, soon!

WAUGH! The door's open!

AAAAAARGHHHH!

Calm down, Scooter, I'm wearing a parachute.

Now pay attention...

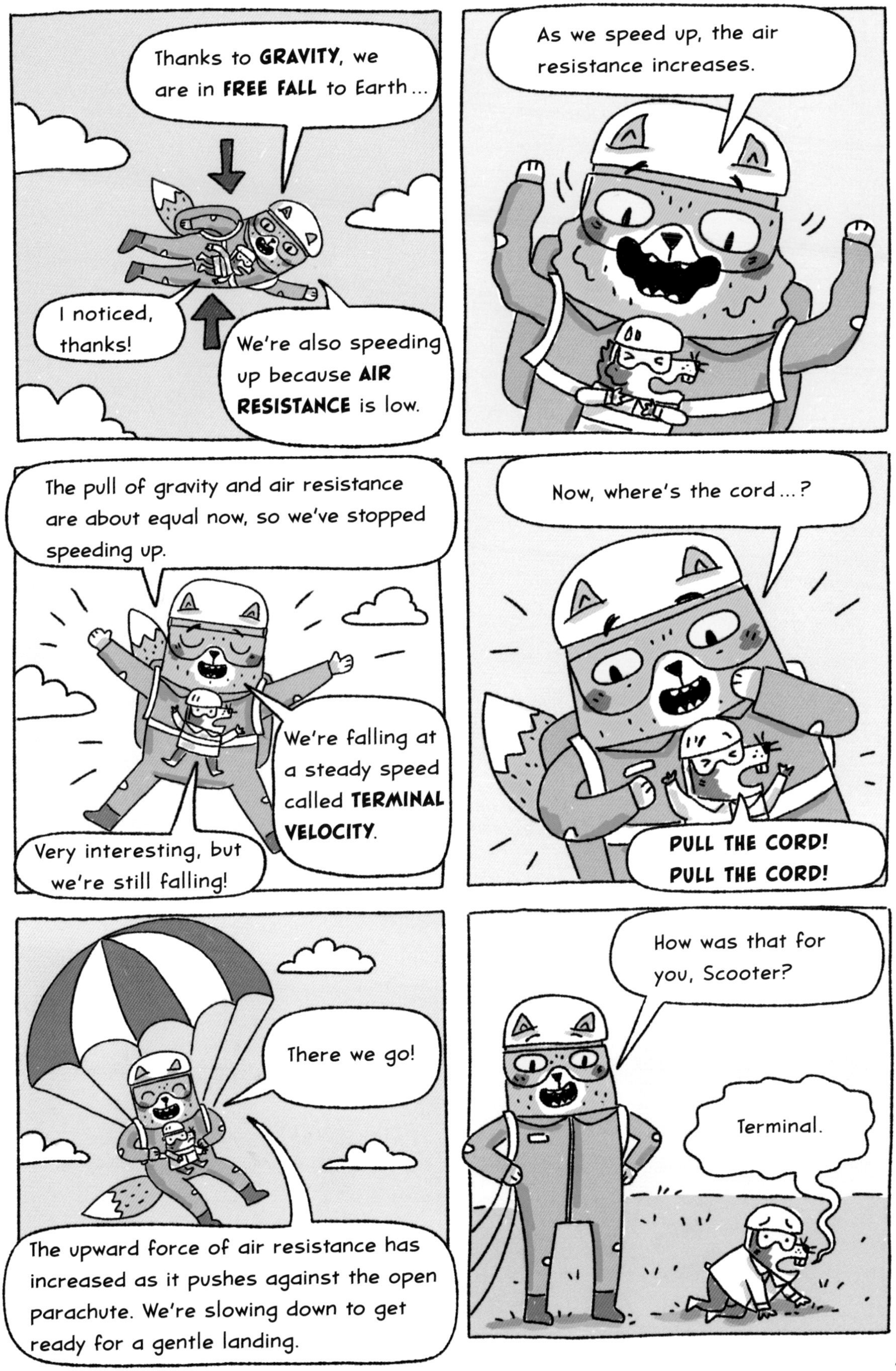

Thanks to **GRAVITY**, we are in **FREE FALL** to Earth...
I noticed, thanks!
We're also speeding up because **AIR RESISTANCE** is low.
As we speed up, the air resistance increases.
The pull of gravity and air resistance are about equal now, so we've stopped speeding up.
We're falling at a steady speed called **TERMINAL VELOCITY**.
Very interesting, but we're still falling!
Now, where's the cord...?
PULL THE CORD! PULL THE CORD!
There we go!
The upward force of air resistance has increased as it pushes against the open parachute. We're slowing down to get ready for a gentle landing.
How was that for you, Scooter?
Terminal.

How to Avoid a Crash

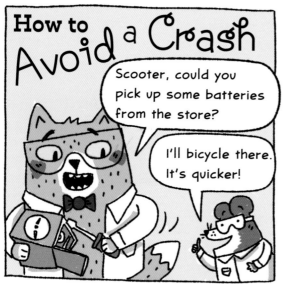

Scooter, could you pick up some batteries from the store?

I'll bicycle there. It's quicker!

Make sure you wear your helmet.

Of course.

When did you last check your bike brakes?

Not sure ...

What's the most important thing to know when you start moving?

Where you're going?

No. It's how to stop!

Your brake pads are worn and need replacing.

When you pick up the batteries, pick up some new brake pads, too.

Good idea ...

I suggest that you walk.

Friction is the force that exists between two objects rubbing together.

Even if a surface looks smooth, there are microscopic bumps on it. It's these bumps catching on each other that cause the **resistance force** called friction.

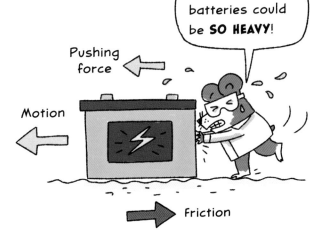

Pushing force

Motion

Nrrrrh! Who knew batteries could be **SO HEAVY**!

Friction

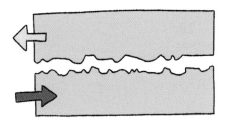

Without friction we would slip about when we walked, and cars would not grip onto road surfaces.

Moving objects are slowed down by friction, and some of their **kinetic energy** is converted into **thermal energy**.

Friction caused by objects moving through a gas or liquid is called **drag**. An aircraft experiences drag from the air during flight.

REEEECH!

Brakes use friction to slow vehicles. Bike brakes push **brake pads** against the metal wheel rim. When the pads touch the rim, friction occurs against the rotation of the wheel, slowing it down.

How to Slip Away

Has this computer become heavier, or have I gotten weaker?

You're trying to push it over a rough surface so there's more **FRICTION**.

You need to use more **FORCE** to move it.

I don't have any more force to give.

Then a little **LUBRICATION** might help.

If I pour oil on the floor, that will reduce the friction, and the computer should slide over it.

This is much easier.

But the oil's getting under my feet, too!

SPLAT!

SQUEEEEE!

Because of **friction**, moving one object over another requires **force**. The smoother the objects, the less friction and the less force is needed to move them.

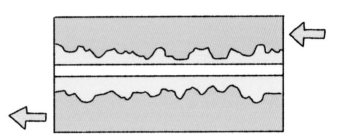

For engines, reducing friction is important. Too much friction means that they need extra energy to operate, metal parts soon wear down, and they can overheat as their **kinetic energy** is converted into **thermal energy**.

A **lubricant** can be used to form a slippery barrier between hard surfaces, reducing friction and wear on the objects rubbing against each other.

Whoaaaaaaa!

Liquids work as lubricants because they can change shape and make a hard, bumpy surface feel smoother. Water can be a lubricant, but engines use **oil** or **grease** because these remain liquid even at high temperatures.

How to Walk a Tightrope

And now the death-defying Scooter the Stupendous is ready to perform his most daring feat yet...

...walking the tightrope!

Excellent landing!

BOING!

If you really want to walk across the tightrope, you need to move your **CENTER OF GRAVITY**.

How can I move **GRAVITY**?

Tightrope walkers carry a pole to help them balance and to lower their center of gravity.

That's much better!

Although Earth's gravity pulls on every particle of an object equally, there is a point in each object where the weight seems to be concentrated. This is called the **center of gravity**.

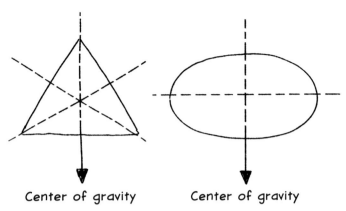

Center of gravity

Center of gravity

Center of gravity is important for **balance**. If you stand up straight, your center of gravity will be in the middle of your body, giving you a **stable** position.

If you carry a weight in one hand, you have to lean to retain balance, moving your center of gravity toward the opposite foot.

Tightrope walkers use a balancing pole to place their center of gravity above the tightrope.

A low center of gravity increases an object's stability. Holding the pole low adds weight below the walker's center of gravity, which makes them more stable.

How to Take Off

WHA?!

Sorry, Professor. I was just testing my plane designs.

Hmm... you could improve this by turning up the wing tips and losing the point on the front...

But, as I'm busy on a very delicate experiment...

I suggest you take your aircraft design outside!

On my way!

To take off, aircraft have to gain enough speed to benefit from the differences in air pressure on the wings in order to gain **lift**.

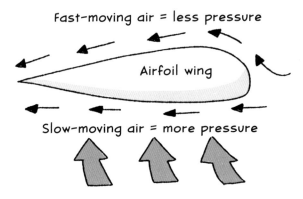

Fast-moving air = less pressure

Airfoil wing

Slow-moving air = more pressure

Aircraft use powerful engines to push them forward. As they gain speed, air moves over and under the wings.

Aircraft wings have an **airfoil** shape, which is more curved over the top than the bottom. Air passes over the wing faster than below it, creating a difference in **air pressure**. Higher air pressure below the wing then pushes the wing up.

Other forces that act on an aircraft are **gravity**, engine **thrust**, and **drag** caused by air resistance.

Lift

Thrust

Drag

Gravity

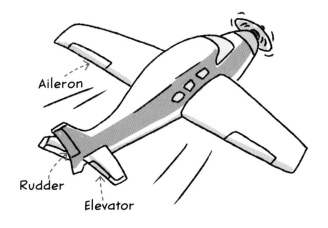

Aileron

Rudder

Elevator

To steer a plane, the pilot controls flaps on the wings (ailerons) and tail (elevators), which change the lift applied to each wing. Moving the tail rudder turns the plane left or right.

Full of Hot Air

Hot-air balloons take off in a different way to winged aircraft.
They take advantage of the fact that hot air rises.

A hot-air balloon uses a
burner to heat up the air
(or other gas) inside the
balloon. Heating the
air makes it expand
to become **less dense**,
while inflating
the balloon.

The only
way is up,
Scooter!

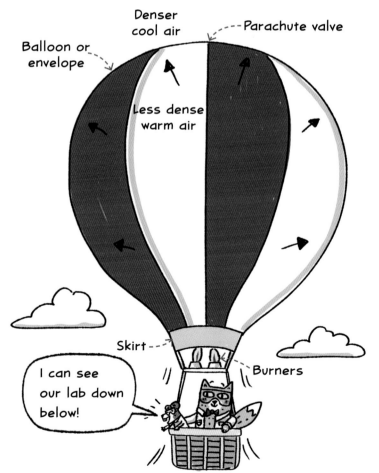

Denser
cool air

Parachute valve

Balloon or
envelope

Less dense
warm air

Skirt

Burners

I can see
our lab down
below!

The hot air is lighter than
the cooler air outside the
balloon. The hot air rises,
creating a **lift force** on
the balloon.

To steer, pilots move the
balloon up and down into
different wind streams.
To return to the ground,
the pilot opens a
parachute valve to
release some hot air.

Electric Tricks

(Electricity, Magnetism)

How to Give Your Hair a Lift

Ahem.

Oh, sorry, Scooter. Didn't see you there.

If you really want to give your hair a lift, Scooter, I have just the thing...

How embarrassing.

This is a Van de Graaff generator.

Ooh!

Try putting your paws on it.

It works using static electricity!

It's hair-raising!

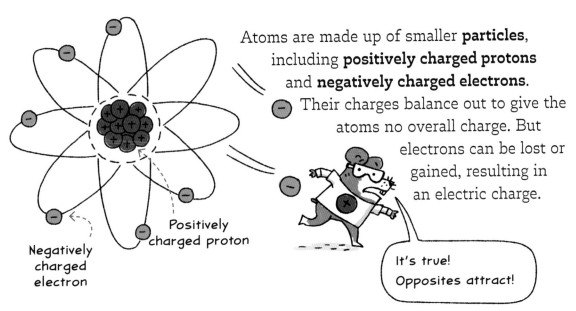

Atoms are made up of smaller **particles**, including **positively charged protons** and **negatively charged electrons**. Their charges balance out to give the atoms no overall charge. But electrons can be lost or gained, resulting in an electric charge.

Positively charged proton

Negatively charged electron

It's true! Opposites attract!

This can be demonstrated by rubbing a balloon against a wool sweater. Some electrons jump from the balloon, and as opposite charges attract, the balloon sticks to the sweater. This buildup of electric charge is called **static electricity**.

A Van de Graaff generator builds up static electricity with a spinning belt, and a charge collects on its metal dome. When you touch it, you gain the charge. As the same charges repel, your hairs push apart and stand up.

An example of static electricity is seen during storms when water droplets rub together to build a huge negative charge at the bottom of clouds. This is discharged as lightning to an oppositely charged point, such as another cloud, a tall building, or the ground.

How to Be Positive

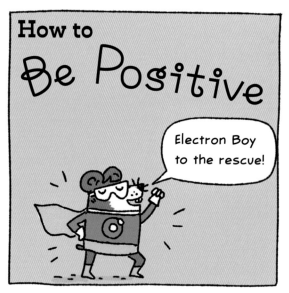

Electron Boy to the rescue!

"Electron Boy," I need your help to make this light bulb work!

Is that all? I was expecting a more exciting mission.

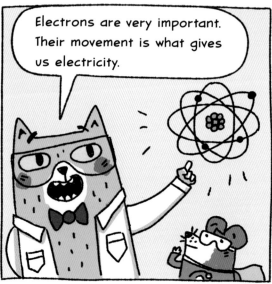

Electrons are very important. Their movement is what gives us electricity.

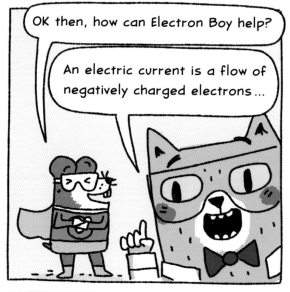

OK then, how can Electron Boy help?

An electric current is a flow of negatively charged electrons...

So you need me to get moving?

That's exactly right!

This is not what I had in mind when I decided to be a superhero...

Unlike **static electricity** an **electric current** is a moving flow of **negatively charged electrons**.

An **electric circuit** is a path that allows an **electric charge** to move and provide the energy to power gadgets and turn on lights. A simple circuit features a battery, a loop of wire, and a light bulb.

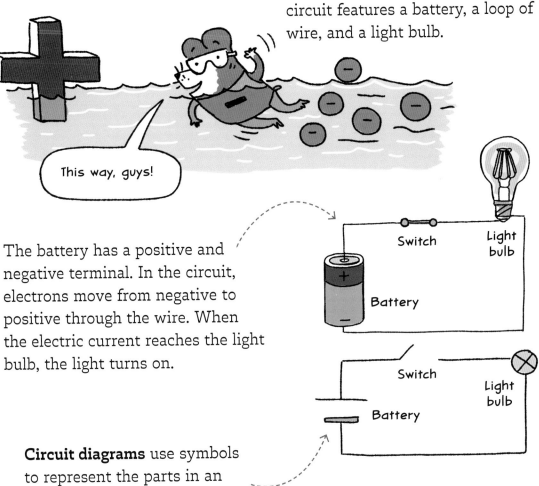

This way, guys!

The battery has a positive and negative terminal. In the circuit, electrons move from negative to positive through the wire. When the electric current reaches the light bulb, the light turns on.

Switch

Light bulb

Battery

Switch

Light bulb

Battery

Circuit diagrams use symbols to represent the parts in an electrical circuit.

They can get very complicated.

I'm **POSITIVE** this will work!

How to Use Potato Power

CATCH!

Are we having fries for dinner?

No. We're going to use the potatoes for power.

Awww.

Are they supposed to look like rabbits?

Those are electrodes.

Ta-da! We have electricity!

Can we use it to make fries?

Batteries have two terminals, a negative and positive **electrode** separated by a solution called an **electrolyte**. The terminals are made of different metals—such as copper and zinc. Copper attracts electrons from the zinc, and they move through the electrolyte to build a difference in charge between terminals.

It won't fit into my alarm clock.

You can't switch clock batteries with potatoes!

When the battery is connected to an electrical circuit, the movement of electrons produces electrical energy.

Electrons

Zinc electrode

Copper electrode

Electrolyte

Electrolyte

Lemons and potatoes include an acid that can work as an electrolyte. When electrodes are pushed into the potatoes and connected in a circuit, electrons can move though the acid to produce electricity.

Batteries have a limited life. Once the electrons stop moving, the batteries no longer provide energy.

Don't eat the potatoes after they've been used as batteries!

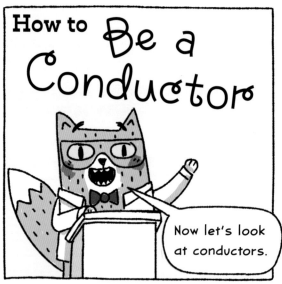

How to Be a Conductor

Now let's look at conductors.

Ahem.

♪Electricity goes with electron flows.♪

That's a plastic baton. It's no good for conducting!

You need copper wire!

You should have said...

♪For a flow good and proper, you need to use copper!♪

Conductors are materials that allow electricity (the flow of electrons) to pass through easily.

The wires used to connect power supplies to electrical gadgets, and the wires used in light bulbs are all conductors.

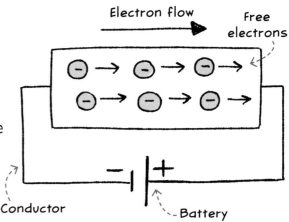

Electron flow

Free electrons

Conductor

Battery

Good conductors include the metals copper, steel, iron, gold, and silver. These all have a large number of free electrons that can move between atoms.

The opposite of conductors are **insulators**, which do not allow electricity to pass through. The atoms in insulators keep a tight hold of their electrons.

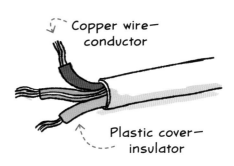

Copper wire— conductor

Plastic cover— insulator

Plastic is a good insulator. It is used to wrap electrical wiring and prevents you from getting an electric shock. Other insulating materials include rubber, glass, wood, and air.

How to Be More Attractive

64

Magnetism is an invisible force that can push or pull materials. Like an electric current, this is due to the movement of electrons.

Individual atoms can act like tiny magnets. Mostly, the atoms point in random directions so the little magnets cancel each other out. But in some materials, such as iron, all the atoms can line up in the same direction and so the iron becomes magnetized.

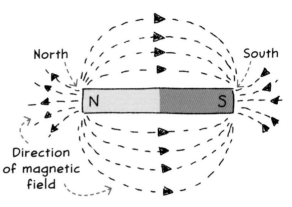

North

South

N

S

Direction of magnetic field

Magnets have **two poles**, with the magnetic force flowing from **north** to **south**.

When **opposite poles** come into contact, they **attract** each other.

When poles that are the same come too close, they **repel** each other.

Earth acts like a giant magnet, too. Thanks to its molten iron core, it has a magnetic north and south pole!

That's why compass needles point north!

How to See a Magnetic Field

Would you like to see a magnetic field?

I thought magnetic fields were invisible.

They are. But you can see their effect. Here's what you need...

Paper

Bar magnet

Iron filings

Place the paper over the magnet, then sprinkle iron filings over it. Give the paper a tap to nudge the filings.

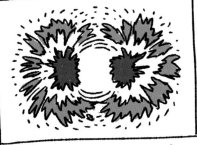

Whoa! They've formed a pattern!

The filings have been attracted and repelled by the magnetic force in the magnet.

The pattern the iron filings form follows the direction of the magnet's magnetic field.

The filings are gathered most tightly around the magnet's poles, where the magnetic field is strongest.

If you could see it, the Earth's magnetic field would look similar to the field around a magnet but would reach far into space. Earth's magnetic poles are close to the geographic poles that the Earth spins around.

Earth's magnetic field protects us from solar wind—charged particles that come from the Sun.

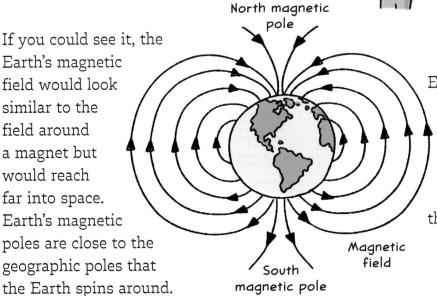

North magnetic pole

South magnetic pole

Magnetic field

How to Hover

Professor, these magnetic levitation boots don't seem to work.

That's because the powerful magnets in the boots are attracted to the metal. You need magnets that repel.

Repelling magnetic forces are used in maglev trains to make them hover over rails.

Maglev trains?

This is my mini maglev!

Oooh!

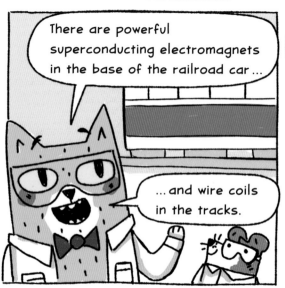

There are powerful superconducting electromagnets in the base of the railroad car...

...and wire coils in the tracks.

As the car passes over the rails, the coils become magnetized. The car and rails repel each other just enough to lift the train.

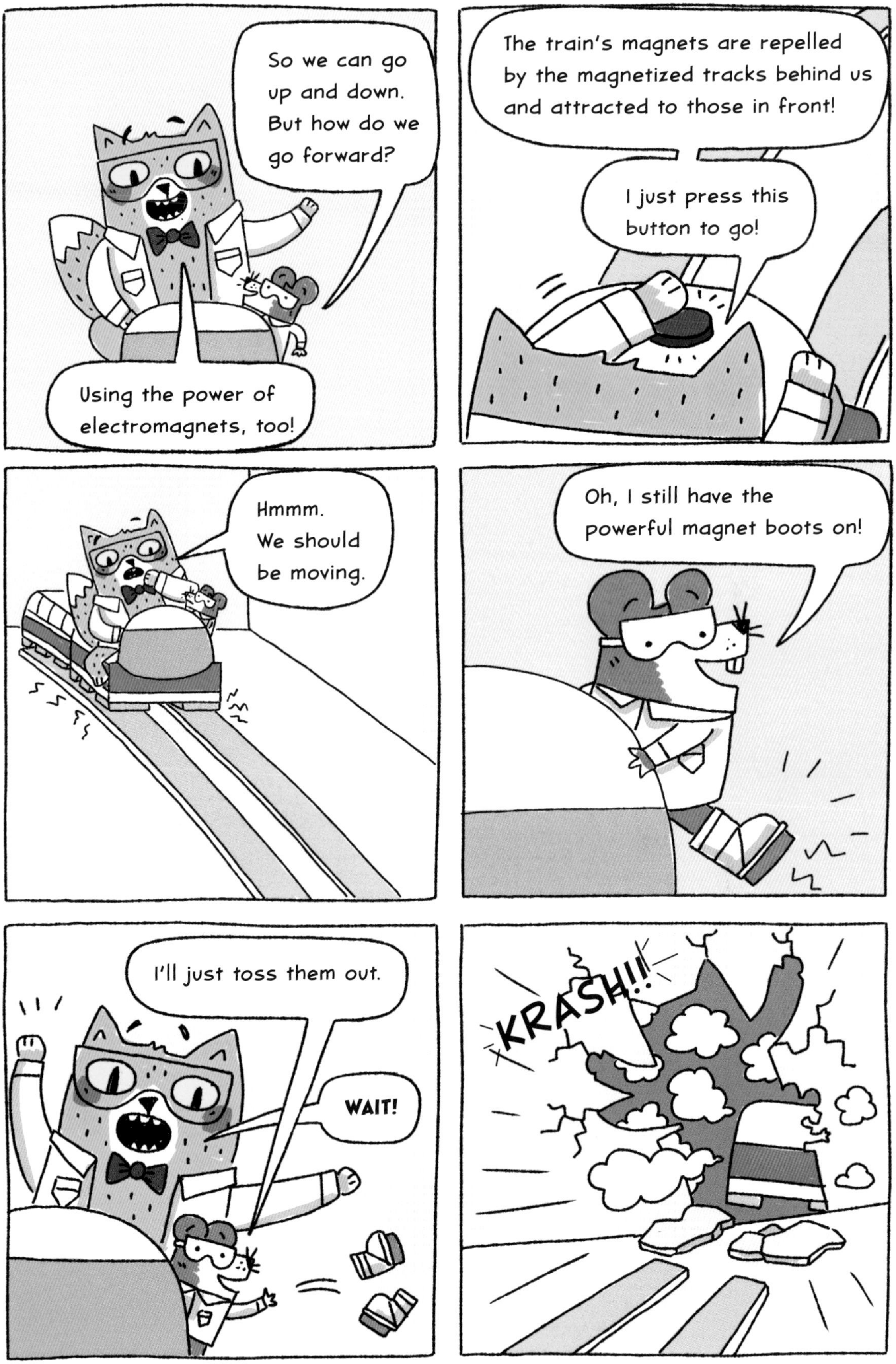
So we can go up and down. But how do we go forward?
Using the power of electromagnets, too!
The train's magnets are repelled by the magnetized tracks behind us and attracted to those in front!
I just press this button to go!
Hmmm. We should be moving.
Oh, I still have the powerful magnet boots on!
I'll just toss them out.
WAIT!
KRASH!!

How to Make Chips

Scooter, do you have the supplies I requested?

Right here, Professor!

The whole bag is full of snacks!

I thought we might work up an appetite.

I asked for *microchips*.

Yes, I got cheesy ones.

Microchips are circuits used in all the computers and gadgets we use.

Oh.

Microchips are even used to keep track of pets by implanting a tiny chip under the animal's skin.

The chip can be scanned to find the animal's name and address.

I might forget shopping lists, but I do remember my name!

Microchips are miniature electronic circuits that control most modern gadgets from smartphones to microwave ovens and computers.

The **circuits** are etched onto a tiny square of **silicon** that could fit on your fingertip.

What's silicon?

Silicon is a made from a special kind of sand that is heated, purified, then shaped into very thin wafers.

Patterns are **etched** onto the silicon wafers by covering the silicon with a **light-sensitive material** called **photoresist**, then shining light on it through a **stencil**.

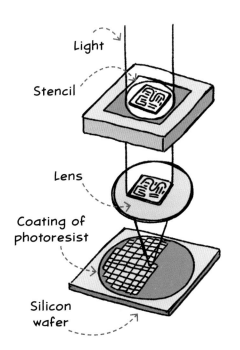

Light

Stencil

Lens

Coating of photoresist

Silicon wafer

The pattern on the silicon acts as a guide for adding chemicals and metals that give the chip the ability to perform specific tasks. A microchip can have many layers of patterns— even a hundred of them!

Chips ahoy!

Square chips are cut from the wafer and coated with protective glass or plastic.

How to Test for Intelligence

Are you ready for the intelligence test, Scooter?

Not really ...

Don't worry, Scooter. It's not you being tested. It's the computer's artificial intelligence!

Phew! That's a relief.

I want you to talk to the computer as if it were a person.

Then I'll check its responses.

Try asking the AI a question.

What does AI stand for?

AI stands for "artificial intelligence."

It spoke! Cool!

Hi, AI, why do you never see pigeon babies?

Maybe ask it some intelligent questions.

Artificial intelligence (AI) is the ability of computers to learn and problem solve like we do. AI can duplicate many human tasks. It can read, play games, create images, and even drive cars.

AI can study information and respond quickly. While computers can't feel emotions, they can mimic our way of talking. AI is already used to answer questions online and over the phone.

Computer programmer Alan Turing developed a test to find out if an AI could pass as human. In the test, questions are fed into a computer and answered by both a human and the AI. If the questioner can't tell which is which, the AI has passed the test.

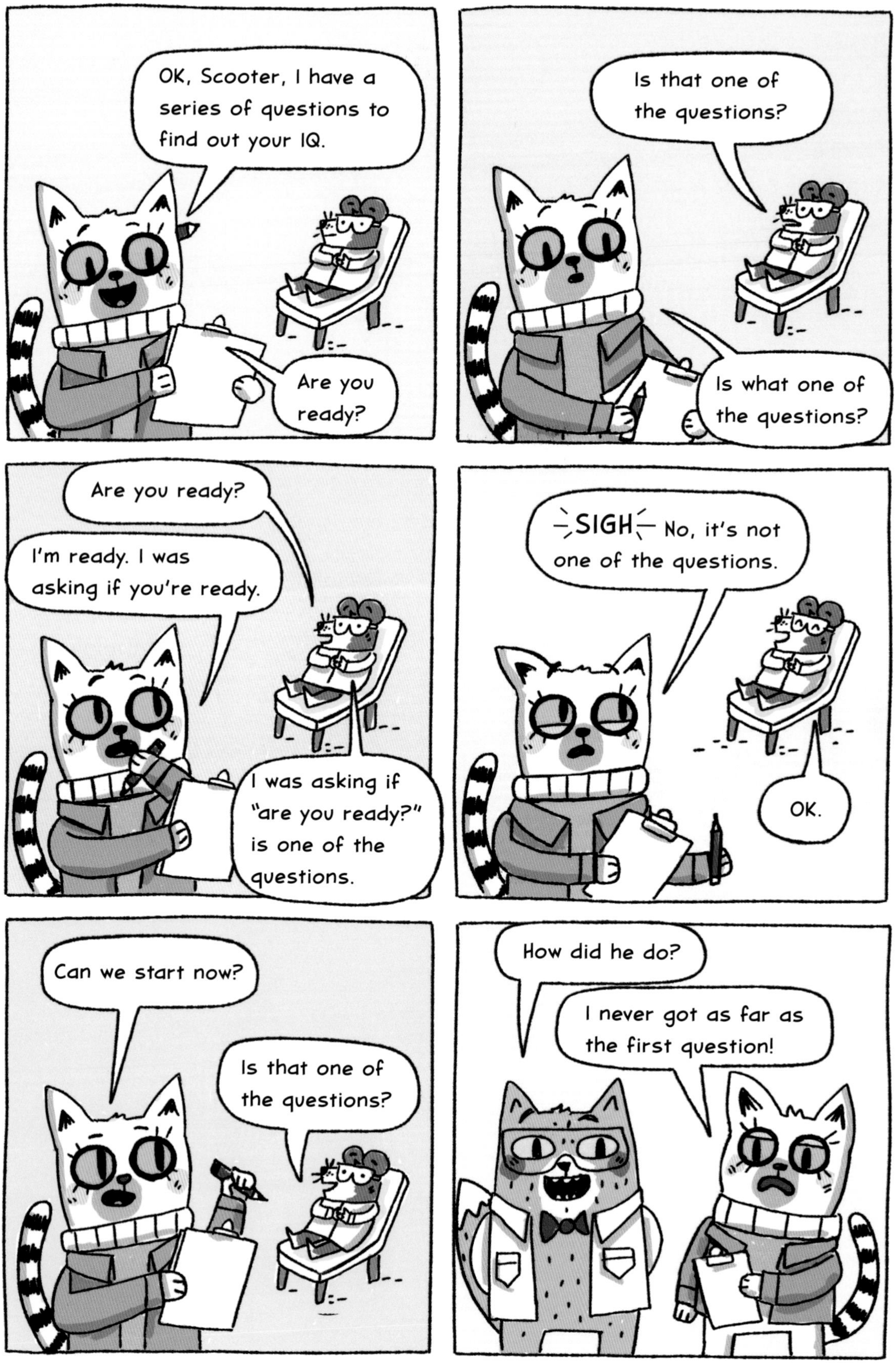
OK, Scooter, I have a series of questions to find out your IQ.
Are you ready?
Is that one of the questions?
Is what one of the questions?
Are you ready?
I'm ready. I was asking if you're ready.
I was asking if "are you ready?" is one of the questions.
SIGH No, it's not one of the questions.
OK.
Can we start now?
Is that one of the questions?
How did he do?
I never got as far as the first question!

Out of This World

(Space Physics)

How to Move at Superspeed

GO!

But ...

You're not moving!

Oh, but I am, and so are you ... at **SUPERSPEED**!

I don't FEEL very fast.

It may not feel like it, but we're all on the move with the Earth.

The planet is spinning at 1,670 km/h (1,038 mph)*.

Now, you're making my head spin!

*at the equator.

The Earth is also moving around the Sun at about 30 km (19 miles) per second!

Somebody grab the brake!

And the Earth and solar system are orbiting the galaxy at 220 km (137 miles) per second.

Now, THAT's superspeed!

I need to sit down. All this racing around has worn me out!

The Earth rotates on its axis relative to the Sun every 24 hours—that's a day!

We can't feel the spin because everything around us is moving at the same speed.

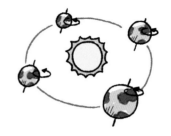

Why don't we fly off into space if the Earth is moving so fast?

GRAVITY keeps us grounded.

The planet would need to speed up and spin at 28,437 km/h (17,670 mph) for us to be thrown off into space.

Over a year, the Earth makes one loop of the Sun. The solar system is positioned on one arm of our galaxy, the Milky Way, and that is spinning around its center, too.

Even the Milky Way is on the move, racing through space at about 600 km (360 miles) per second.

THE MILKY WAY

The solar system

How to Get into Orbit

Are you following me, Scooter?

I'm in your **ORBIT**, like a satellite!

You're getting under my feet!

I need to rest.

You can't stop moving and stay in orbit!

Pant   Pant

You're right! I'm being pulled in by the **FORCE OF GRAVITY**!

Gravity is an invisible force of attraction between all objects that have mass. The more massive the object, the greater its gravitational pull.

Earth is pulled toward the Sun, but our planet's forward motion balances with the Sun's gravity to keep it in an elliptical orbit around the Sun. It is the same for the Moon in orbit around Earth.

To put a satellite in orbit around Earth, a rocket must launch with a **thrust** greater than the force of gravity. A rocket will reach a speed of 4,950 km/h (17,800 mph) on its way up above Earth's atmosphere.

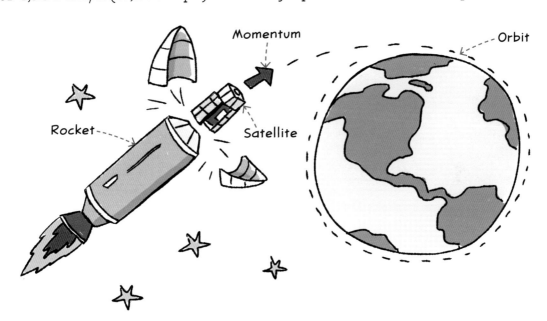

Momentum

Orbit

Rocket

Satellite

When the rocket reaches its planned height, the satellite is released. The satellite continues moving forward in a curved path that balances with the pull of gravity.

The pull of gravity is stronger the closer you get to Earth, so satellites in close orbit must travel faster than those farther away.

How to
Walk on the Moon

This is one small step for a guinea pig...

All your steps are small, Scooter.

I'm pretending to walk on the Moon, Professor.

No need to pretend. Let's do this properly.

We're going to the Moon?! Hooray!

Sorry, no, but I've built this **LOW-GRAVITY CHAMBER** to reproduce the effects of being on the Moon.

I still want to go to the real Moon one day.

First you need a space suit for protection and to keep you at a comfortable temperature.

The backpack carries your air and power supply.

It feels heavy.

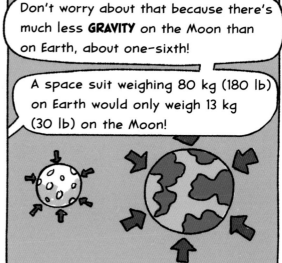

Don't worry about that because there's much less **GRAVITY** on the Moon than on Earth, about one-sixth!

A space suit weighing 80 kg (180 lb) on Earth would only weigh 13 kg (30 lb) on the Moon!

Now, let me change the gravity setting...

Astronauts find it easier to do short jumps rather than walk on the Moon.

It's true! I feel much lighter!

But be careful, Scooter!

Whoaaaaaa! I'm leaving the Moon!

You won't be able to jump off the Moon, but you could jump six times higher, and land badly...

I didn't know the Moon was going to be so bouncy!

Oof!

How to See the Universe

WOW!

Let me see! Let me see!

Can't see anything yet. I'm just amazed at how dirty the lens is.

Right, now we can do some stargazing.

Which constellation shall we look at? The Great Bear? The Bull? The Swan? The Ram? The Scorpion...?

What's the matter, Scooter?

Is there no Guinea Pig constellation?

When we look up on a clear night, we can see stars that are light-years away. But to see more of the Universe we need help.

Telescopes use **optics** (lenses and mirrors) to collect light from dim and faraway objects and magnify it. There are two types of telescopes— **refracting** and **reflecting**.

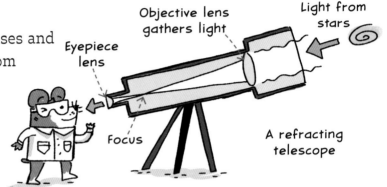

Objective lens gathers light

Light from stars

Eyepiece lens

Focus

A refracting telescope

Refracting telescopes use a large **objective lens** at the end of a tube to collect light. The light is **refracted**, or bent, to a focus near the back of the tube, then sent to a small **eyepiece** lens where it is magnified for viewing.

Reflecting telescopes gather light using mirrors. The light is focused and bounced to a smaller mirror, which reflects it toward the eyepiece.

Light from stars

Eyepiece lens

Small mirror reflects light toward eyepiece

Primary mirror gathers and reflects light

To see the farthest objects, we need telescopes that can detect not just visible light but other parts of the electromagnetic spectrum, such as radio waves, X-rays, and infrared radiation.

How to See Behind a Star

How many stars are in the Universe, Professor?

About 200 billion trillion. I haven't counted them all.

I bet there are even more hiding behind other stars.

We can see some of them, too!

How?

Using **GRAVITATIONAL LENSING**.

Gravity is an invisible force of attraction between all objects that have mass. The more massive an object, the greater its gravitational pull. Stars can be really massive and have such strong gravity that they can even bend or magnify light from distant galaxies.

Light normally travels in a straight line, but it can be bent around a massive object, such as the core of a galaxy. This sometimes produces more than one image of a distant object.

I'm seeing double.

Gravitational lensing also magnifies the light from distant objects, so telescopes can detect objects normally out of their range.

The bending of light can also tell astronomers that there is a massive object, such as a **black hole**, close by, producing a very strong gravitational pull.

YUM!

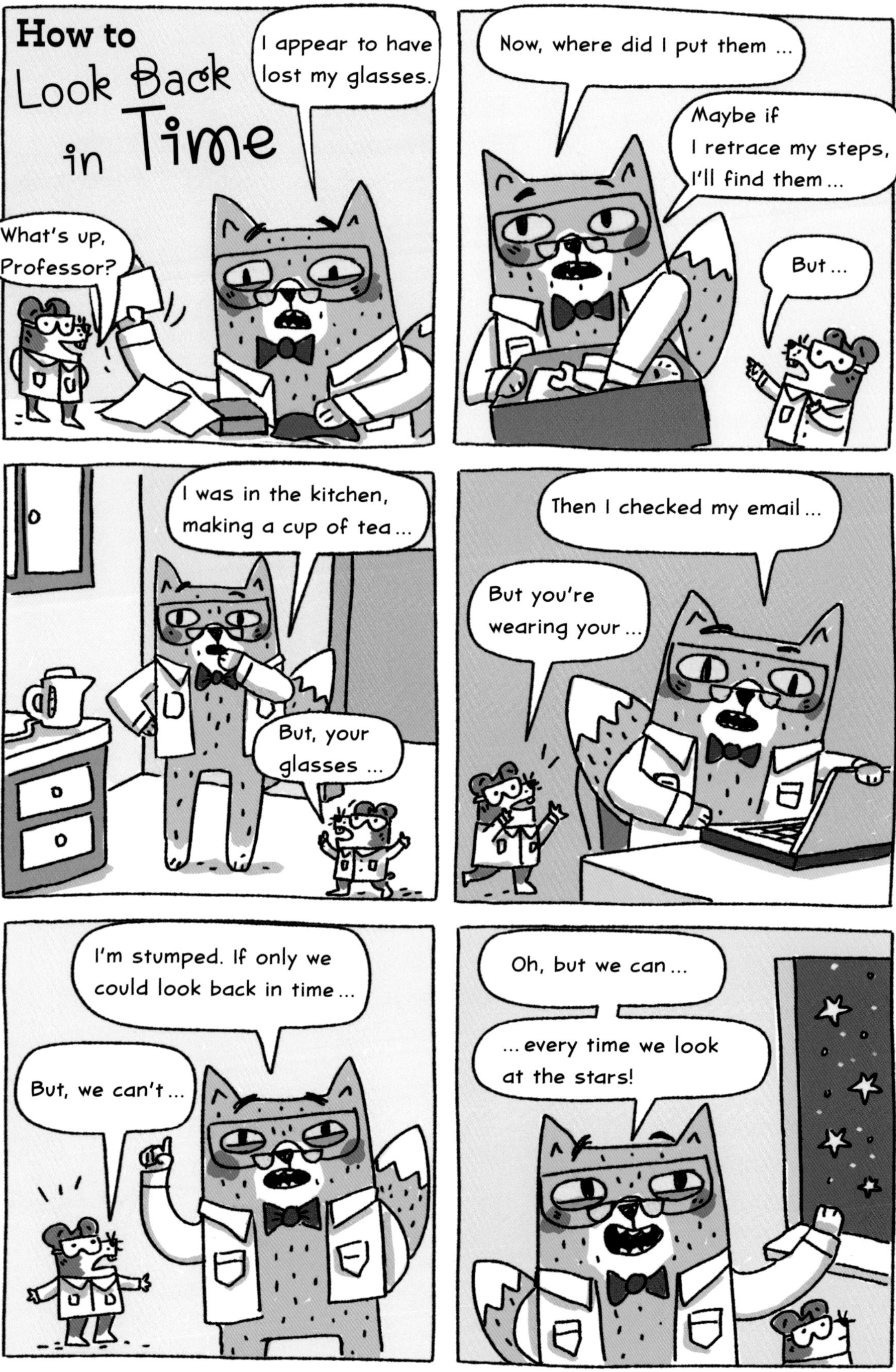
How to Look Back in Time
I appear to have lost my glasses.
What's up, Professor?
Now, where did I put them ...
Maybe if I retrace my steps, I'll find them ...
But ...
I was in the kitchen, making a cup of tea ...
But, your glasses ...
Then I checked my email ...
But you're wearing your ...
I'm stumped. If only we could look back in time ...
But, we can't ...
Oh, but we can ...
... every time we look at the stars!

Distances in space are so huge that we have to measure them in **light-years**. A light-year is the distance that light—the fastest thing in the Universe—travels in one year. One light-year equals 9.46 trillion km or 5.88 trillion miles.

Light from the Andromeda Galaxy takes 2.5 million years to reach Earth.

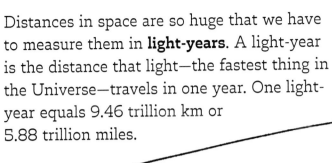

Light from the Sun takes 8 minutes to reach Earth.

Light from the next-nearest star takes 4.3 years to reach Earth.

The light we see from distant objects in space may be billions of years old by the time it reaches us. By the time we see a star, it might have died already!

If a star is 100 light-years away from Earth, we're seeing the light that left it 100 years ago. The **Andromeda Galaxy** is the most distant object we can see with the naked eye.

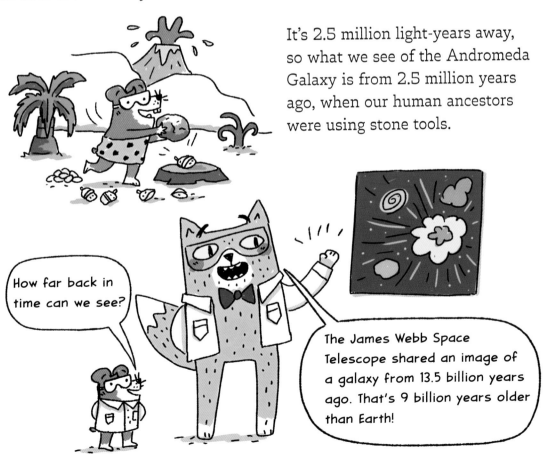

It's 2.5 million light-years away, so what we see of the Andromeda Galaxy is from 2.5 million years ago, when our human ancestors were using stone tools.

How far back in time can we see?

The James Webb Space Telescope shared an image of a galaxy from 13.5 billion years ago. That's 9 billion years older than Earth!

The Long and the Short of It

The length of the day and night changes through the year due to the tilt of the Earth.

The Earth travels around the Sun over **365.25 days (a year)** and spins on its **axis** over **24 hours (a day)**, but its axis is tilted at an angle of **23.5 degrees**.

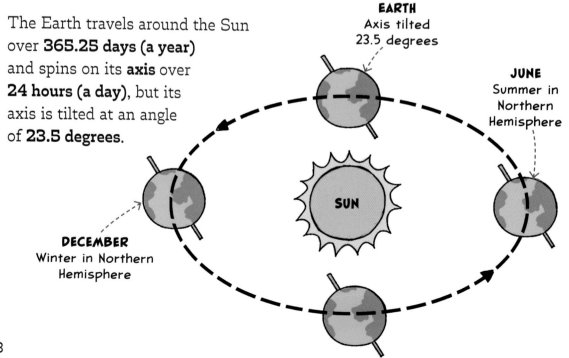

EARTH
Axis tilted
23.5 degrees

JUNE
Summer in Northern Hemisphere

SUN

DECEMBER
Winter in Northern Hemisphere

This means that different parts of the world are pointed more toward the Sun than other parts during the year. When a hemisphere (half of the Earth) is tilted toward the Sun, it's warmer and summertime. For the hemisphere tilted away from the Sun, it's colder and wintertime.

When a hemisphere is at its maximum tilt, this is called the **solstice**.

Do the days change by the same amount for everyone?

No. Around the **EQUATOR**, days and nights stay the same length all year round, 12 hours of day and 12 hours of night.

For the Northern Hemisphere, summer solstice is around June 21.
This is the longest day of the year, with the most sunlight.

What about the **POLES**?

At the poles, you can get weeks of sunlight and weeks of darkness at some times of the year!

Brrr! I'd need extra fur!

Winter solstice is around December 21. This is the shortest day of the year, with the least sunlight.

How to Measure Space

That's a very long tape measure, Scooter.

You said we were going to measure outer space.

There's no tape long enough to measure distances in space! You're talking **LIGHT-YEARS**!

How can you measure distances if you can't go there?

Using the **PARALLAX** method!

Hold up a finger at arm's length and look at it with one eye closed.

Now look at it with the other eye.

My finger moved against the background.

That's **PARALLAX**, how objects appear to change position when you change viewpoint.

We can use this to find out how far away stars are.

Do you need to borrow my finger?

For objects in our Solar System, such as the Moon and planets, scientists can bounce radio waves off their surfaces. By measuring the time it takes for the radio waves to bounce back, they can figure out how far away the planets are.

Measuring distances in the rest of our galaxy and beyond is more difficult, but scientists can work out approximate distances in several ways, including using the **parallax method**.

Just as you see a shift of position when you view a raised finger through one eye then the other, astronomers can see small differences in their view of distant stars as Earth moves around the Sun.

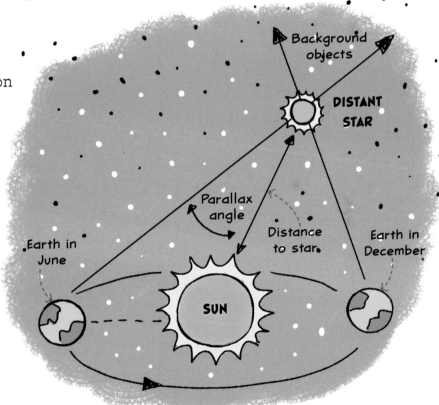

Astronomers look at a target star and its background over months. Knowing the position of Earth, they can calculate the angle that the star appears to move by over a year and use geometry to work out its distance from Earth.

How to Time Travel

Professor, do you think I'll ever become big and brainy like you?

Let's travel into the future and find out!

Are we really going to travel into the future?

That's exactly what we're doing.

So, when do we start?

We haven't stopped! We're already a few seconds into the future since you asked your first question.

I was hoping to jump ahead.

Take a peek at the end of the book if you're in a hurry.

It may appear that we are all moving through time at the same speed, but time isn't the same everywhere.

It is thought that the faster you travel, the slower you experience time than someone standing still.

Time is also affected by **gravity**. Clocks closer to Earth's gravitational pull tick more slowly than those farther away. Clocks on satellites orbiting Earth gain about 40-millionths of a second a day!

Time travel might be possible through **wormholes** or shortcuts through **space-time** (space and time together), but no one has found one yet.

While time travel may be possible, it seems unlikely that you could travel to the past. If you could go back and change the past, it would change the future you left!

Why is Space So Silent?

What are you listening to, Professor?

I said what are you list—

WAUGGH!

You made me jump, Scooter.

I was listening for signals from outer space.

Can I listen?

Go ahead.

I can't hear anything!

Exactly! That's because sound doesn't travel through space!

Sound travels as waves of vibrating molecules. It needs a medium such as air or water to travel through.

When you play music on a stereo, the speakers vibrate, creating changes of pressure in the air. You can feel this with your hand near a loud speaker.

Your eardrums receive the changes in pressure, which your brain translates as sound. The more air molecules that are compressed, the louder the sound.

But outer space is a **vacuum**, which means there is nothing that sound can travel through. If a nearby star went **supernova**, there would be a huge explosion, but you wouldn't hear a thing.

WHOOOOM!

This is good news. If we could hear the Sun's nuclear reactions from Earth, it would be like a continuous roar at 100 decibels. That's as loud as a motorcycle and would damage our hearing!

How Fast is the Universe?

On your marks, get set...

GO!

It's no good, Professor, no matter how fast I run, I can't beat the beam of light.

pant Pant

I knew you wouldn't.

Nothing can move faster than the speed of light.

Let me try something.

If I wear a headlamp when I run, my light will be faster than your light!

The fastest thing in the Universe is light. Light moves at 300,000 km (186,000 miles) per second. At this speed, you could zip around the Earth 7.5 times in one second.

Why can't anything go faster than light?

Because to go faster would require **UNLIMITED ENERGY**.

To make an object speed up requires energy. As an object moves faster its mass increases. At near light speed this mass becomes infinitely large. Speeding it up would mean using unlimited or **infinite** energy!

So, nothing can go faster than light?

186,000 mi/s

Well, there is something ... the **UNIVERSE ITSELF**!

While the relative speed between two objects cannot be faster than the speed of light, there is no limit on the expansion of space.

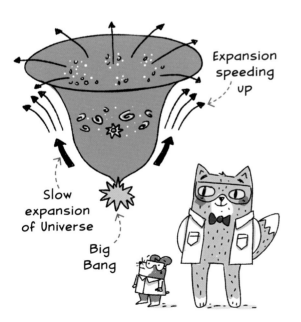

Expansion speeding up

Slow expansion of Universe

Big Bang

When the Universe began, it ballooned in size at a speed faster than light, and it is still expanding.

Space telescopes have picked up light from a few million years after the Universe began. But because space is expanding faster than light, we can't see the Universe's first light, as it's moving away faster than the light can reach us!

How to End the Universe

Gasp!

What is it, Scooter?

It's Dr. Destroy! He's invented a machine that could blow up the whole Universe, and Rodent Boy can't stop him!

Ah! A comic book.

Well, that's nothing to worry about. It's just a story.

The Universe is not going to end for billions of years. And we certainly won't be around to see it.

How is the Universe going to end?

Well, there are several ideas about that.

A mysterious force called **DARK ENERGY** is making the Universe expand faster and faster.

If it continues, the stars will end up far apart, run out of fuel, and no new stars will replace them.

The Universe will be mostly dark and cold in a **BIG FREEZE** over about one **GOOGOL** year.

One googol?

1000000000000000000000000
0000000000000000000000000
0000000000000000000000000
0000000000000
0000000000
000000000

A googol is one plus 100 zeros.

I don't like the sound of the Big Freeze. Is there a better end?

How about the **BIG RIP**?

Like that time you split your jeans?

This is a rip you couldn't repair.

The Big Rip sees dark energy pull everything apart. Galaxies break up, stars and planets drift free. Eventually, even **ATOMS** break apart!

Don't like that, either. Can I have another choice?

How about the **BIG CRUNCH**?

Ooh, like my **BREAKFAST CEREAL**?

In the Big Crunch, the Universe starts to shrink as gravity pulls it back.

Galaxies crash into each other, and everything heats up.

Eventually, the whole Universe gets squeezed into a tiny, tiny space.

That doesn't sound nice, either!

What do you expect?! It's the end of the Universe!

I was hoping for a happy ending.

Well, one idea is that after the Big Crunch there's a **BIG BOUNCE**.

That sounds more fun.

The Big Bounce has the Universe shrink to almost nothing, then it explodes in a new **BIG BANG**, rebooting the Universe.

So we could just bounce back and start again?

Yes but that's ages away ...

AND WE'RE ONLY JUST GETTING STARTED!

Riding a Wave

(Waves)

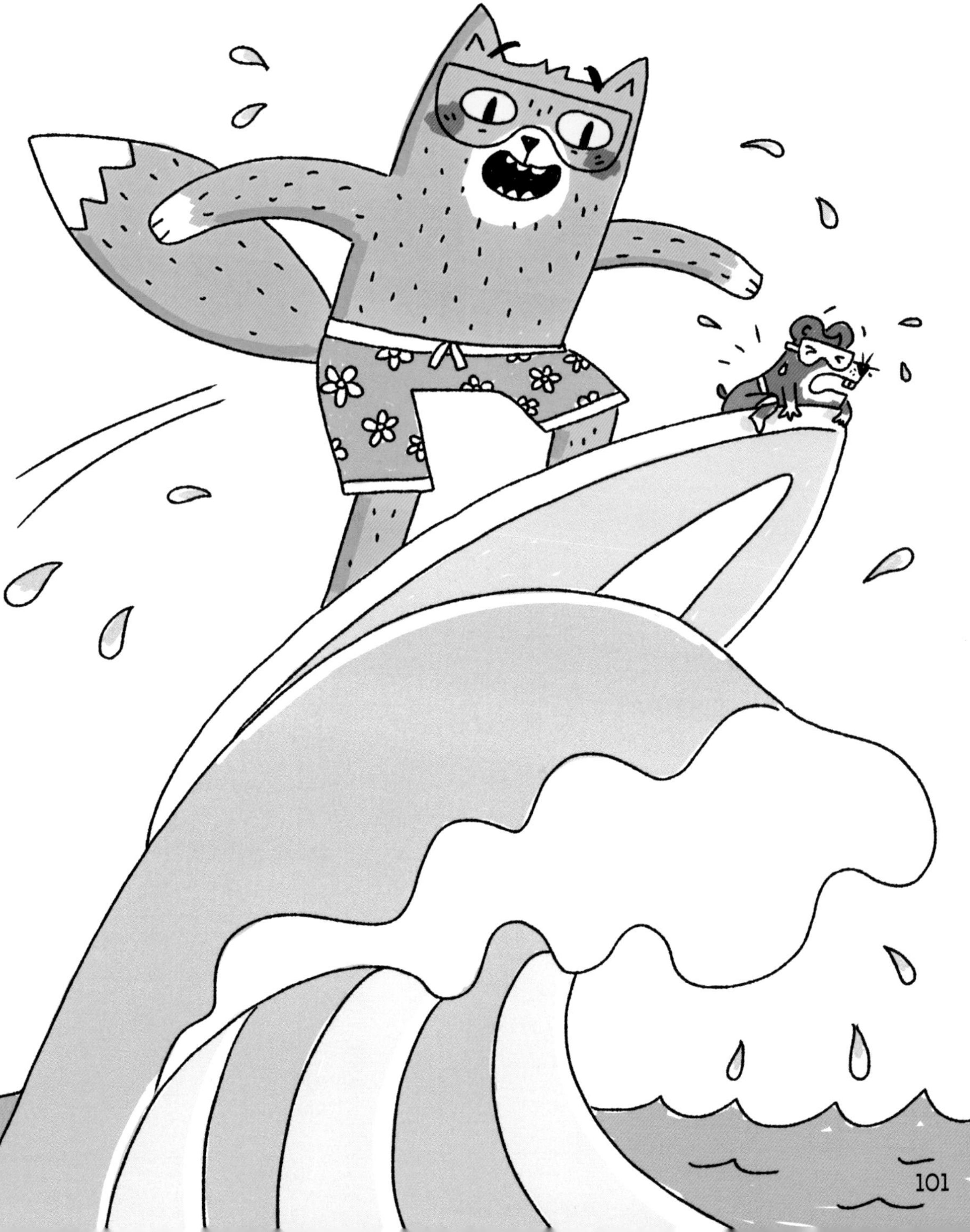

How to Create Waves

Ready, Scooter?

I'm turning on the **WAVE MACHINE** now. Wave level 1!

Wave level 2!

PUFF! PUFF!

Wave level 3!

PUFF! PUFF! How many levels **ARE** there?

Um, 10.

That's me **WAVING** goodbye, then!

Waves are vibrations that move energy from one place to another. Some, like sound waves, need a medium to travel through. Others, like light waves, can travel through space. All of them behave in a similar way.

There are two types of waves: **transverse** and **longitudinal**.

Transverse waves move up and down as they move forward. Light and ocean waves are transverse.

Longitudinal waves squeeze and stretch as they move forward. Sound waves are longitudinal.

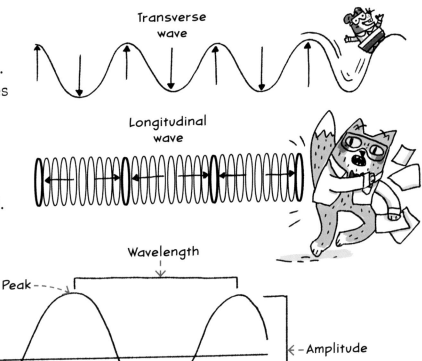

Transverse wave

Longitudinal wave

Peak

Wavelength

Amplitude

Trough

A transverse wave can be shown as a series of **peaks** and **troughs**. The distance between peaks is the wave's **wavelength**. The height of a peak above a central line is the wave's **amplitude**. This is a measure of how much energy the wave is transferring.

Less **AMPLITUDE**, please!

How to Bend a Spoon

I have a challenge for you, Scooter.

Can you bend a spoon without **TOUCHING** it?

I think so...

CLANG–ANG–ANG!

You can't throw the spoons on the road to be squashed by traffic!

Oh.

I had a more subtle solution in mind.

I'll drop the spoon in the glass.

What do you see?

The spoon is **BENT**!

Exactly! This effect is called **REFRACTION**!

Sorry about the rest of our spoons.

When light travels from one transparent medium to another, it changes speed and direction. This is called **refraction**. Refraction is why a swimming pool may appear shallower than it is and why an object dipped in water appears crooked.

When light passes into a **more dense** transparent material, such as from air to glass, the **wavelength** of the light becomes shorter, and it changes its path, turning away from the surface. When the light passes back into a **less dense** material, it regains its speed and bends back toward its original path.

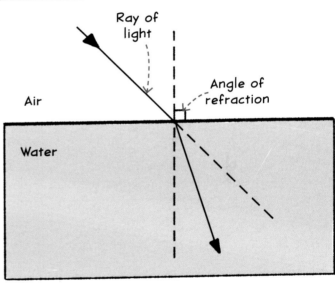

Ray of light

Air

Water

Angle of refraction

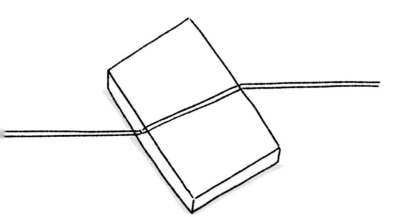

The refraction of light is a property used in the production of lenses for magnifying glasses, telescopes, and microscopes.

How to Make a Rainbow

Now, that's a handsome rainbow!

A **RAINBOW**?!

We have to hurry, Professor!

Hurry?! Where to?

Don't you know? There's a pot of **GOLD** at the end of the rainbow!

But Scooter, even if there was, you'd never find the end of the rainbow!

It's an optical effect caused by sunlight passing through the rain, not a solid thing.

Aww, I guess I'm not going to be wealthy.

Scooter, look up. Just enjoy the riches of this view.

Sunlight is made of different **wavelengths**. The wavelengths we can see are called the **visible spectrum**.

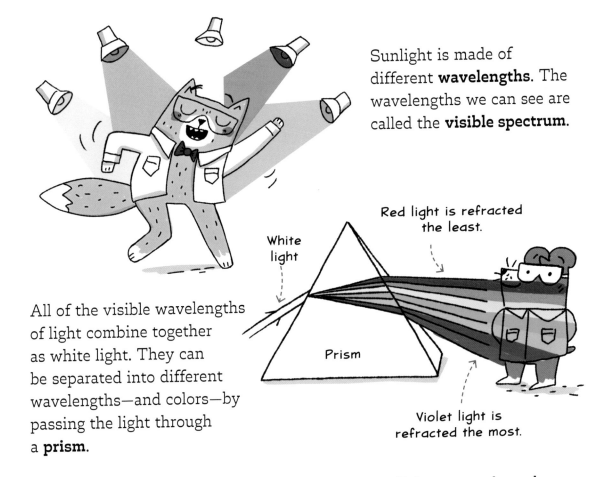

Red light is refracted the least.

White light

Prism

Violet light is refracted the most.

All of the visible wavelengths of light combine together as white light. They can be separated into different wavelengths—and colors—by passing the light through a **prism**.

A prism is triangular-shaped piece of glass. When light passes through it, it bends, or **refracts**. Short wavelengths are refracted more than long wavelengths, and a rainbow of colors is produced.

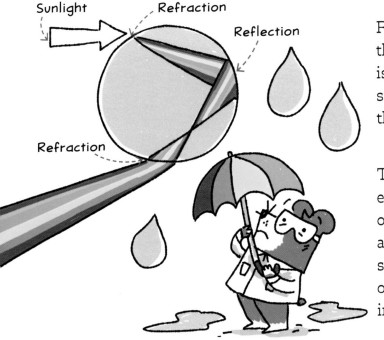

Sunlight

Refraction

Reflection

Refraction

Rainbows are the result of the same process. When rain is followed by sunshine, the sunlight passes through the water droplets in the sky.

The light is refracted when it enters the raindrop, reflected off the back and refracted again into the familiar spectrum of colors: red, orange, yellow, green, blue, indigo, and violet.

Spectacular Spectrum

So, Scooter, do you know there are more colors than those we see in a **RAINBOW**? But you can't see them.

That's helpful!

The **EM SPECTRUM** includes waves with really short and really long **WAVELENGTHS**.

The visible spectrum is part of a larger spectrum of energy waves called the **electromagnetic (em) spectrum**.

Gamma rays are high-energy waves that can pass through almost anything. In space, they are released by superhot objects, such as neutron stars. On Earth, they come from radioactive sources.

X-rays can pass through skin and muscle but are absorbed by bones and metal. They are used by doctors and dentists to produce images of your skeleton and teeth, and to scan luggage at airports.

Gamma rays

X-rays

Better safe than sorry!

Ultraviolet

We can't see **ultraviolet waves**, but we receive them from the Sun. UV rays are the cause of suntans and sunburn.

Infrared radiation is produced by hot objects, and night-vision cameras can reveal it. Astronomers use special telescopes to receive infrared images from space to discover distant stars and galaxies.

The **visible spectrum** is the "white light" we see every day. It is made up of many different colors.

Microwaves are used in roadside speed cameras, satellite signals, and microwaves ovens, where they vibrate molecules to heat up food.

Radio waves have the longest wavelengths. They are used for communication and Internet signals, and they can even travel through space.

Infrared signals are also used in **REMOTE CONTROLS**.

Visible spectrum

Infrared

Microwaves

Radio waves

How to See Skeletons

Scooter, I'm missing a red ball bearing. I need it for the gearing on my hypergizmatic machine.

Ball bearing? Is it **SO** big?

Yes. Have you seen it?

Does it look like a piece of candy?

Oh no, Scooter. You haven't swallowed it have you?

I may have.

We need to take an X-ray to find out.

Lie perfectly still.

There it is!

I guess I'll have to wait until it becomes available...

X-rays are a form of **electromagnetic radiation** with high energy and a short wavelength. They can pass through materials such as skin and muscle and can be used to capture images of what's inside.

X-rays are absorbed by different materials at different rates. They move through soft body parts but are absorbed by hard body parts, such as bone and teeth. Doctors and dentists can use X-rays safely to record images on special film.

In an X-ray image, the hard parts appear white against black, so bone breakages and tooth cavities can be spotted.

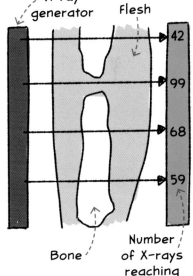

At airports, X-ray scanners are used to check luggage contents. The X-rays highlight solid objects, such as metal items.

Scientists use special telescopes to receive X-rays from distant objects in space, such as very hot objects and black holes.

How to Explore the Microverse

WOW!

What is it, Professor?

You have to see this!

But I'm too small to get up there.

Don't worry about being small, Scooter. Some amazing things are tiny. Just take a look through this **MICROSCOPE**!

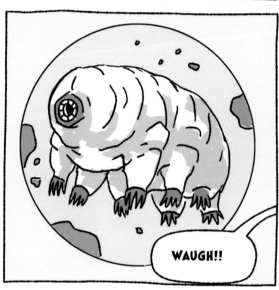

WAUGH!!

What is it?

It's a **TARDIGRADE**, a tough and tiny creature that's almost indestructible.

I'm glad it's really small!

Magnifying glasses and microscopes help us see really tiny objects by using **lenses**.

Lenses are specially shaped pieces of glass or plastic that **refract** (bend) light.

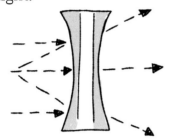

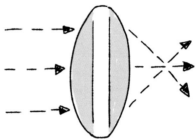

A concave lens refracts light outward.

A convex lens refracts light inward.

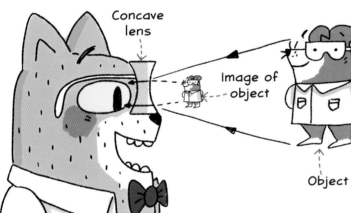

Concave lens

Image of object

Object

Concave lenses are used in glasses for people with nearsightedness who see distant objects to be blurred. The lens focuses an image of distant objects at the back of the viewer's eye.

Convex lenses magnify a view and are used in telescopes and microscopes. In a **microscope**, the subject for viewing is placed on a slide above a light source. Wheels move a series of convex lenses up and down to focus the image in the eyepiece.

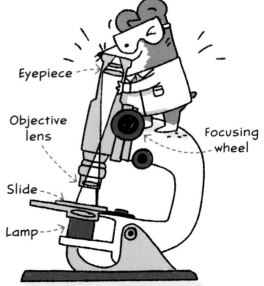

Eyepiece

Objective lens

Focusing wheel

Slide

Lamp

How to Make a Sonic Boom

OK back there?

I'm feeling a little queasy, actually.

We haven't taken off yet!

OK, Scooter, we're approaching a speed of 1,060 km/h (660 mph).

A little more acceleration and we'll **HIT** Mach 1.

Hit?! Don't crash!

Mach 1 is a **SPEED**, Scooter, the **SPEED OF SOUND**.

Will you still hear me screaming?

Don't scream, Scooter.

As we approach the speed of sound, sound waves at the front of the jet are being **SQUEEZED** together.

At Mach 1, the sound waves merge together, until...

BOOM!

BOOM!

AAAIIIIEEEE! What was that?

That was me imitating a **SONIC BOOM**, a shock wave caused by the squeezed sound waves.

We can't hear it in the jet because we're moving too fast.

But it can be heard from the ground.

BOOM!

Talking of the ground...

...can we go back there now?

Emojis for Everyone

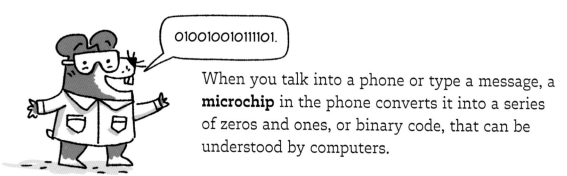

Professor, I have a question.

I'm listening.

I'll message you on my smartphone.

Smartphones are minicomputers that use **radio waves** to send or receive calls and messages. Like all parts of the **electromagnetic spectrum**, radio waves travel at the speed of light.

010010010111101.

When you talk into a phone or type a message, a **microchip** in the phone converts it into a series of zeros and ones, or binary code, that can be understood by computers.

Emojis are digital images that describe objects or moods. They also have to be converted into code to be sent over the phone network. The code also contains details about your phone, so the receiver can identify you.

The radio waves from a smartphone cannot travel far. They are received by a nearby **base station**.

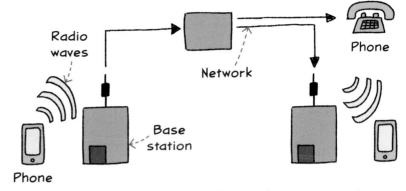

The base station directs your call or message through the phone network to another base station and the destination phone. This happens in an instant, even if the call has to travel around the world.

Smartphones also feature a GPS (**Global Positioning System**) receiver that uses radio waves to communicate with orbiting satellites to pinpoint your location.

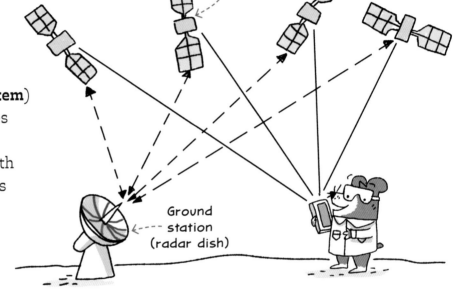

The satellites' location is tracked by a **ground station**. By measuring the time it takes for a signal to come from each satellite, your position can be calculated accurately.

How to Keep Your Cocoa Warm

There's nothing better than a warm cup of cocoa on a winter's day, eh, Scooter?

Mine's gone cold.

Ah, that'll be **HEAT TRANSFER**. The heat is leaving the cocoa through **CONDUCTION**, **CONVECTION**, and **RADIATION**.

How can I stop it?

You need an **INSULATOR**. You could make a foam sleeve for your mug.

Or, you could invest in a **VACUUM FLASK** which uses a vacuum as an **INSULATING LAYER** to keep a liquid hot or cold inside.

That sounds awfully complicated. Is there an easier way?

You could always drink your cocoa faster!

Heat energy travels from hot to cooler objects. It moves in three ways—**conduction**, **convection**, and **radiation**.

Conduction is the movement of heat energy through solids. As a solid gets warmer, its atoms vibrate. This vibration passes through the material, spreading the heat.

If you put a cold spoon in a hot liquid, the spoon gets hot as heat energy is transferred from the liquid to the spoon.

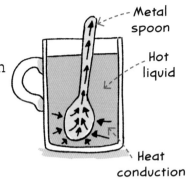

Metal spoon

Hot liquid

Heat conduction

THERMALS are what gliders, balloons, and birds use to gain height.

Cold air

Thermal

Convection is the movement of heat energy through liquids and gases, such as our oceans and atmosphere.

Radiation is the movement of heat by electromagnetic waves. This is how heat from our Sun travels across space to reach Earth—as infrared radiation.

Materials that allow heat energy to transfer quickly are called **thermal conductors**. A metal frying pan is a good thermal conductor.

Materials that slow the transfer of heat energy are called **thermal insulators**. These include plastic, wool, and water. Clothes keep us warm by trapping insulating layers of air next to our bodies.

How to Keep the Noise Down

THUMPA! THUMPA! THUMPA! THUMPA!

Scooter!

Hi Professor! I'm learning to play the drums.

I can see that. I can hear it, too.

THUMPA! THUMPA! THUMPA!

I appreciate you learning a new skill, but I can't work upstairs with the racket.

I can try playing softer.

No, what we need is some **SOUNDPROOFING**.

This **FOAM** will help.

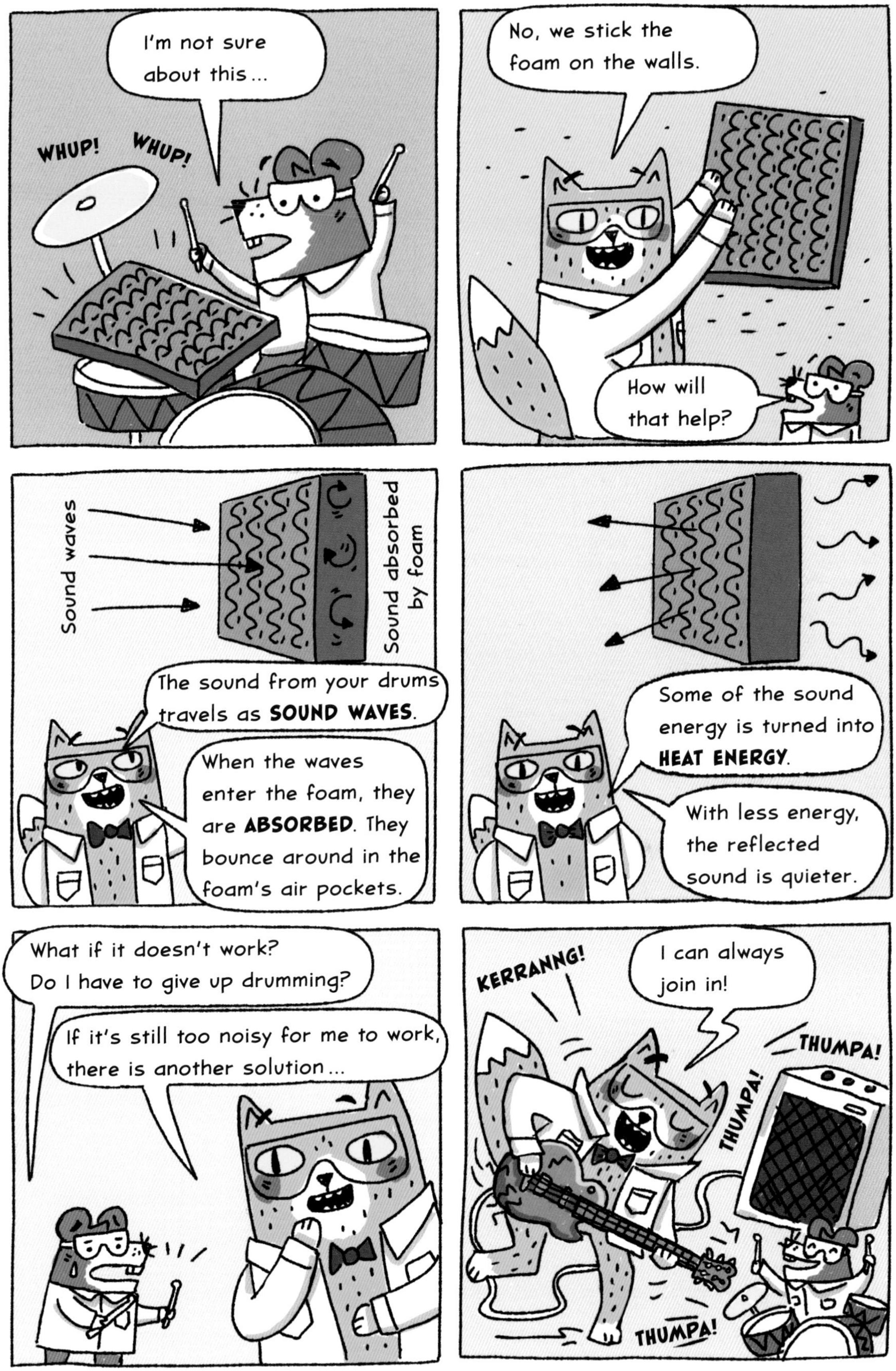
I'm not sure about this...
WHUP! WHUP!
No, we stick the foam on the walls.
How will that help?
Sound waves
Sound absorbed by foam
The sound from your drums travels as SOUND WAVES.
When the waves enter the foam, they are ABSORBED. They bounce around in the foam's air pockets.
Some of the sound energy is turned into HEAT ENERGY.
With less energy, the reflected sound is quieter.
What if it doesn't work? Do I have to give up drumming?
If it's still too noisy for me to work, there is another solution...
KERRANNG!
I can always join in!
THUMPA!
THUMPA!
THUMPA!

How to Look Around Corners

Hi, Scooter!

How did you know it was me?

I can see around corners!

You have **SUPERPOWERS**?!

No, I put up a **CONVEX MIRROR** in the corner.

It shows me a reflection of whoever arrives at the door.

Scooter? Where are you?

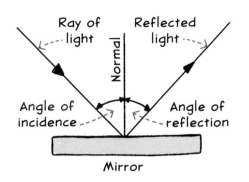

Ray of light — Reflected light

Normal

Angle of incidence

Angle of reflection

Mirror

If it wasn't for **reflections**, we would only see light sources like the Sun and lamps. It is the light reflected from objects that we see.

Most objects have rough surfaces, so light bounces off them in many directions. **Mirrors** are very smooth, so they reflect a clear image.

A ray of light hits a mirror at an **angle of incidence**, measured from a right angle to the mirror called the **normal**. The light bounces away from the mirror at its **angle of reflection**. Both of these angles are the same.

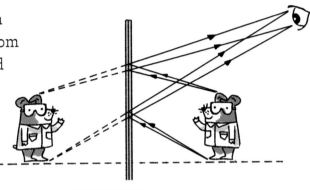

Why is everything flipped **LEFT TO RIGHT** in a mirror?

The reflection is not left to right but **BACK TO FRONT**!

The image you see in a mirror is a virtual image that appears to be the same distance away from the mirror as the object reflected.

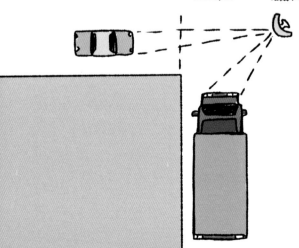

Curved **CONVEX MIRRORS** make it possible to see around corners. These are used near road "blind spots" to show drivers what is approaching around a bend.

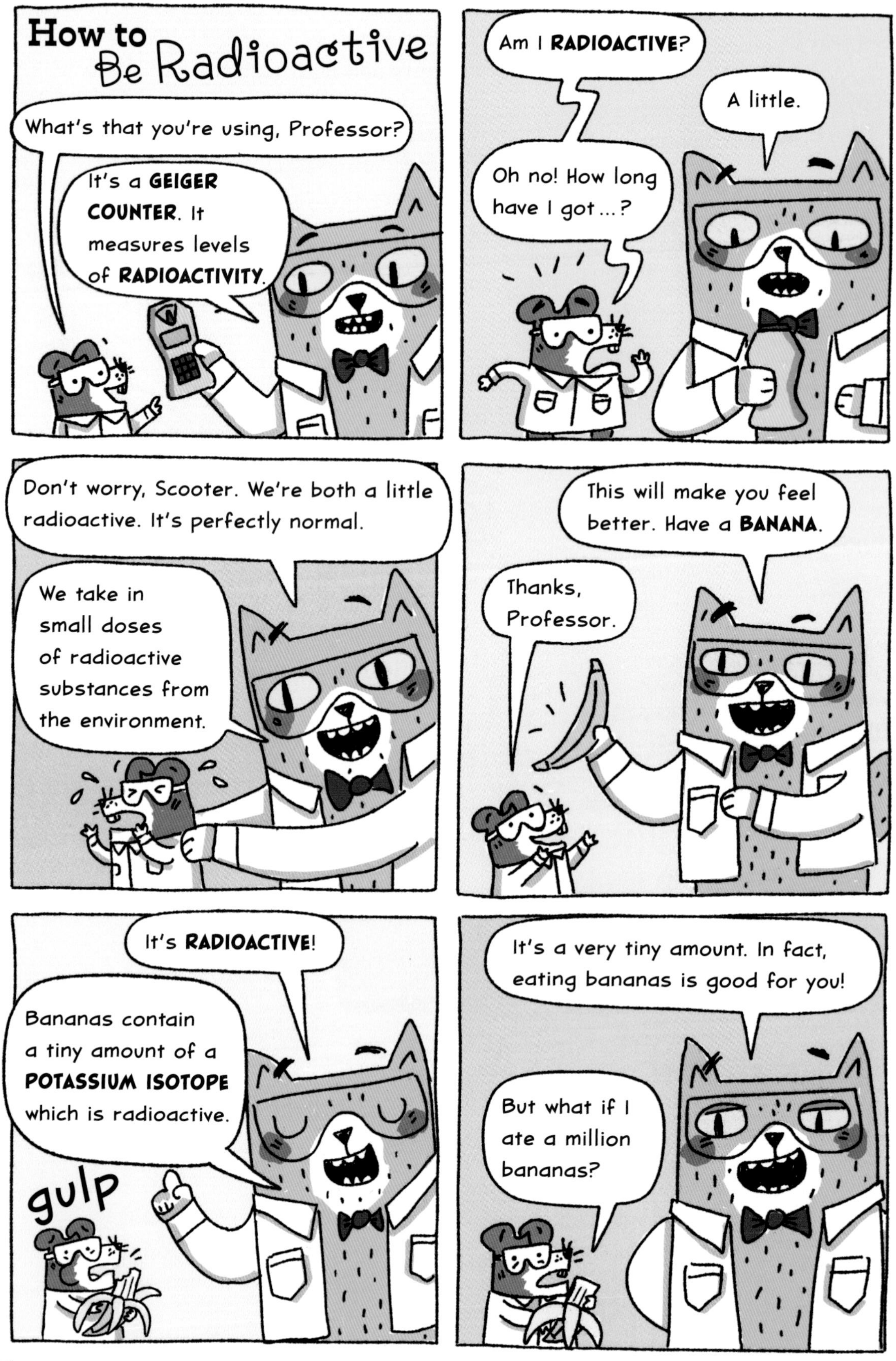
How to Be Radioactive
What's that you're using, Professor?
It's a GEIGER COUNTER. It measures levels of RADIOACTIVITY.
Am I RADIOACTIVE?
A little.
Oh no! How long have I got...?
Don't worry, Scooter. We're both a little radioactive. It's perfectly normal.
We take in small doses of radioactive substances from the environment.
This will make you feel better. Have a BANANA.
Thanks, Professor.
It's RADIOACTIVE!
Bananas contain a tiny amount of a POTASSIUM ISOTOPE which is radioactive.
gulp
It's a very tiny amount. In fact, eating bananas is good for you!
But what if I ate a million bananas?

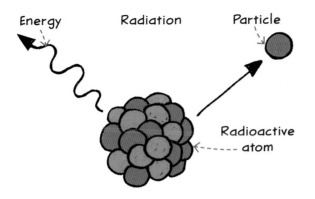

Energy Radiation Particle

Radioactive
atom

The atoms in most elements are stable, but in **radioactive** elements they change over time, releasing particles and energy as radiation.

While some radioactive elements can be dangerous and cause cancer, some naturally radioactive atoms are not harmful in small doses.

Several foods contain traces of radioactivity, particularly those high in the element **potassium**. These include bananas, Brazil nuts, carrots, and potatoes. But this is nothing to worry about.

A typical adult human body contains about 140 g (5 oz) of potassium. A tiny proportion of this is the isotope **potassium-40**, about 280 times the amount you would find in one banana. This radioactive material in your body is not harmful. Our bodies need potassium.

Radioactivity can be useful. Doctors use some forms of radiation to kill germs.

Scientists measure the amount of a radioactive form of **carbon** to figure out the age of fossils, while the radioactive element **uranium** is used to produce nuclear energy.

How to Be a Singing Star

And now, performing for the first time on this stage, put your hands together for...

Scooter!

Thank you.

I can't hear you!

There appears to be a problem with your microphone.

Something's wrong...

Try it now.

TAP

TAP

HELLO!

Microphones are devices that turn sound waves into electrical signals.

Sound waves are vibrations of molecules. When you sing into a microphone, the vibrations you produce pass through the air and hit a thin sheet in the microphone called a **diaphragm**.

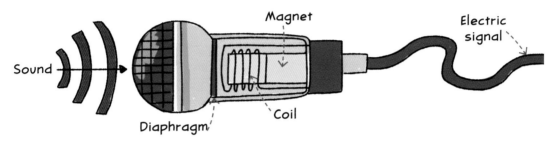

Magnet

Electric signal

Sound

Diaphragm

Coil

In many microphones, the diaphragm is connected to a coil around a magnetic field. The moving diaphragm and coil produce an electric signal.

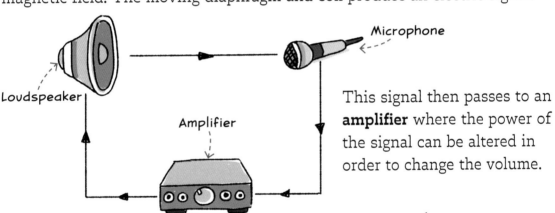

Microphone

Loudspeaker

Amplifier

This signal then passes to an **amplifier** where the power of the signal can be altered in order to change the volume.

The signal then travels to a **loudspeaker** where the electric signal is turned back into vibrations in the loudspeaker's cones. These vibrations pass through the air as sound waves. In this way, your singing can be heard at different volumes.

Index